DATE DUE

JAPANESE AUTO TRANSPLANTS IN THE HEARTLAND

Corporatism and Community

SOCIAL INSTITUTIONS AND SOCIAL CHANGE
An Aldine de Gruyter Series of Texts and Monographs
EDITED BY
Michael Useem • James D. Wright

JAPANESE AUTO TRANSPLANTS IN THE HEARTLAND
Corporatism and Community

ROBERT PERRUCCI

ALDINE DE GRUYTER

New York

About the Author

Robert Perrucci is professor of sociology at Purdue University. He is author or editor of eleven books and has published over sixty research articles and book chapters on topics related to political economy, work, and organizations. His most recent books published by Aldine de Gruyter are *Plant Closings: International Context and Social Costs*, and *Networks of Power: Organizational Actors at the National, Corporate and Community Levels*. He is currently the editor of *Social Problems*, the journal of the Society for the Study of Social Problems.

ALDINE DE GRUYTER
A division of Walter de Gruyter, Inc.
200 Saw Mill River Road
Hawthorne, New York 10532

This publication is printed on acid-free paper ∞

Library of Congress Cataloging-in-Publication Data

Perrucci, Robert.
   Japanese auto transplants in the heartland : corporatism and community / Robert Perrucci.
      p.   cm.
   Includes bibliographical references and index.
   ISBN 0-202-30528-7 (alk. paper) 0-202-30529-5 (cloth)
   1. Automobile industry and trade—United States—Foreign ownership—Case studies.   2. Corporations, Japanese—United States—Location—Case studies.   3. Middle West—Economic conditions.
I. Title.
HD9710.U52P47   1994
338.8'87292'0973—dc20   93-50053
                                                                                        CIP

Manufactured in the United States of America

10 9 8 7 6 5 4 3 2 1

To Carolyn, my partner,
and to Celeste, Mark, Chris, Alissa
and especially Martin

Contents

Preface

The idea for this book was formed during the early 1980s when I was studying the impact of plant closings on displaced workers and communities. At the same time that some communities were struggling with the high unemployment and reduced revenue that accompanies plant closings, other communities were aggressively competing to attract new business. In one community, workers who were displaced by a plant closing expected to receive retraining funds through the Job Training and Partnership Act (JTPA), only to find that the state had committed all the JTPA funds to train new workers for a Japanese transplant.

Soon it became apparent that deindustrialization, job loss, and economically depressed communities were linked with the escalating interstate competition to provide multimillion dollar incentive packages for businesses to settle in their state. When Japanese automobile companies considered coming to the United States, they fueled the interstate competition for these large projects, which promised thousands of jobs and economic growth.

I would like to thank Richard Child Hill and Michael Useem for their support and encouragement to carry out this project on Japanese auto transplants. They helped me obtain a fellowship from the Center for Research in the Social and Behavioral Sciences at Purdue University, allowing me to devote full time to my research. I am grateful to the School of Liberal Arts for its support of Center Fellowships.

Kathleen Cummings, William C. Green, and anonymous library staff at Middle Tennessee State University and Morehead State University helped in obtaining newspaper coverage about transplants in Tennessee and Kentucky.

My early writings about the political economy of auto transplants benefited from the critical reactions of Patricia Boling, David Caputo, David Fasenfest, Heidi Gottfried, Richard Hogan, Carolyn Perrucci, and Cynthia Stohl.

Robert Eichhorn was the first to read early drafts of the manuscript. His critical reading of the first two chapters helped to clarify the purposes of the book and alter its structure. Carol Bangert read the entire first draft with the critical eye of a journalist who lives in a transplant community.

Finally, I thank Candy Lawson for her special efforts in preparing the several drafts of the manuscript.

                                                                    Robert Perrucci

Chapter 1

The Coming of the Transplants:
Why Are They Important?

It'll be official today: Lafayette gets car plant

This front-page headline appeared in the *Lafayette Journal and Courier* on December 2, 1986. After months of competition among states, representatives of Isuzu Motors, Ltd., and Fuji Heavy Industries, Inc., announced a joint venture to build a Subaru-Isuzu auto assembly plant in Tippecanoe County near Lafayette, Indiana.

On December 27, 1986 the paper published a special edition. The front page in even larger type announced:

SPECIAL REPORT
Introducing Fuji-Isuzu

The stories accompanying these headlines are full of hope and optimism regarding new job opportunities, economic growth, and improvement in the standard of living for people in the area. Similar headlines and stories were found in five other cities in five other states in the region that also became the home for Japanese auto assembly plants, referred to as *transplants*. Between 1982 and 1989 six major Japanese auto assembly plants would begin production in Ohio, Tennessee, Michigan, Illinois, Kentucky, and Indiana. In less than a decade, Japanese companies created an auto industry comparable to those in several Western European na-

1

tions and capable of challenging the Big Three [General Motors (GM), Ford, and Chrysler] in the United States.

The transplant phenomenon in the United States occurred in the context of a changing global economy and the declining strength of the U.S. economy. The dominance of U.S. corporations in steel, autos, coal, and oil production was challenged by other industrialized nations, and resulted in declining profits from the domestic economy between 1965 and 1975. Corporations attempted to maintain their profits by increased investment abroad. Between 1970 and the mid-1980s, capital flows from the United States tripled as major U.S. firms reduced production at home and invested in operations in other countries. At the same time, capital flows to the United States increased tenfold, as foreign direct investment in the United States reached $262 billion in 1987, up from $13 billion in 1970 (Feagin and Smith 1987; Glickman and Woodward 1989). The one indicator of the changing position of the United States in the global economy that received greatest attention in the media was the balance of trade figures. The U.S. trade balance, which had been positive since 1893, first showed a deficit in 1978. The United States reported a $10 billion deficit in 1980, $135 billion in 1984, and a record $170 billion in 1987. The United States had changed its position from the world's largest creditor to the largest debtor nation.

A look behind the general statistics of trade deficits and declining profits revealed a similar pattern in the experiences of the steel, auto, and consumer electronics industries. Once dominated by U.S. firms, these sectors steadily lost market share, profitability, and technological superiority to foreign competition. Among the reasons for the decline in these basic industries are failures of management, demands of labor, and ineffective government policies. Auto industry executives failed to assess the shifting consumer demand for smaller, fuel-efficient cars, and the capabilities of foreign auto firms to meet that demand. Organized labor was able to bargain for inflation-based wage increases unconnected to productivity. And the federal government's efforts to protect threatened industries was usually through haphazardly applying tariffs, quotas, and voluntary restraints, which were often imposed long after they could do any good.

As the U.S. presidential elections approached in November 1980, a climate of concern about the declining U.S. auto industry was receiving almost daily treatment in the media. The public and political mood of the country can be gauged from stories about the U.S. economy that appeared in the *New York Times* throughout 1980.

Early in 1980 the leadership of the Big Three auto firms and the United Auto Workers (UAW) began a systematic two-pronged campaign pressing for restrictions on imports of foreign-made cars and urging the Japanese to open auto plants in the United States.

> UAW President Douglas Fraser says he will ask Congress for legislation requiring Japan to open assembly and parts plants in the United States as a condition for selling vehicles in the American market (*New York Times,* January 14, 1980, IV, 3:1)

> Chrysler chairman Lee A. Iacocca, GM executive Vice President Roger B. Smith and Ford Motor Co. executive Vice President William O. Bourke urge dealers to curb sales of foreign made cars in U.S. (*New York Times,* February 12, 1980, IV, 1:4)

> Chrysler says it might lose as much as $650 million in 1980. Blames increased sale of imported cars and "current economic conditions" for its financial plight. (*New York Times,* March 19, 1980, IV, 5:4)

Japanese automakers expressed great reluctance to build plants in the United States, citing the large investment required by such plants and the negative impact it could have on their profitability. They proposed instead to slow the growth of their exports, as indicated by Toyota President Euji Toyoda, who stated that Toyota Motor Company would limit 1980 exports to the United States to 1979 levels (*New York Times,* February 19, 1980, IV, 2:3). This proposal received a cool response from U.S. auto and labor leaders, since 1979 exports were already at a record high. A joint statement by UAW President Douglas Fraser and Ford Chairman Philip Caldwell called for imports to be cut back to the 1974–1976 level of 900,000 units annually, rather than the 2.1 million cars expected to be imported in 1980.

Officials of two administrations in Washington also put pressure on the Japanese, by indicating that they shared the concerns of U.S. automakers. The U.S. Ambassador to Japan, Mike Mansfield, in a speech to the Japanese Press Club, urged Toyota and Nissan Motor Companies to build auto assembly plants in the United States. Mansfield warned the Japanese that failure to do so would set off protectionist pressures in the United States because of the election year (*New York Times,* January 29, 1980, IV, 4:1). President Carter expressed support for UAW efforts to get foreign automakers to build plants in the United States, and reservations about restricting imports because it would force Americans to buy U.S. automakers' "gas guzzlers" (*New York Times,* April 18, 1980, IV, 2:1). And with the presidential election nearing, Republican vice presidential nominee George Bush, meeting with Japanese government leaders in Tokyo, indicated that the Reagan administration would not rule out the possibility of restrictions on the import of Japanese cars (*New York Times*, August 20, 1980, II, 9:1). This point was soon reinforced by presidential nominee Ronald Reagan, who told a gathering of auto- and steelworkers in Detroit that if elected he would limit exports of Japanese automobiles to the United States (*New York Times*, September 3, 1980, 8:1).

After the Reagan-Bush victory in the November 1980 elections, the U.S. House of Representatives voted 317–57 on December 3 to authorize the president to negotiate curbs on the import of Japanese cars and trucks. Added to this drumbeat of criticism about imports were the voices of governors from states heavily involved in the auto industry, and hearings on imports held by the U.S. International Trade Commission.

It is interesting to note that during this period of intense pressure on the Japanese to build auto plants in the United States, the Big Three automakers were still hard at work closing plants in the United States and moving production abroad. In February 1980, General Motors announced plans to build three auto components plants in Spain, one in Austria, and one in Northern Ireland. These plants were part of GM's ten-year, $20 billion overseas expansion program. And in March 1980, both GM and Chrysler announced the establishment of plants within a duty-free zone in Mexico. These plants were set up under the Mexican *maquiladora* industrialization program, which provided lower wages and production costs to U.S. firms located just inside the Mexican border.

This discussion of news items in the *New York Times* throughout 1980 and early 1981 is but a sampling of the economic and political issues of this period. The domestic auto industry was rapidly losing market share to Japanese imports, and unemployment in the auto and steel industries was at politically unacceptable levels, putting pressure on elected officials for action. Moreover, those declines were not being viewed as isolated problems of an otherwise healthy economy. The American public and its political leaders were becoming increasingly aware of, and ambivalent about, the extent to which foreign investment had penetrated the U.S. economy. Writing in 1988, Martin and Susan Tolchin pointed out that "foreign money has invaded the American economy with an impact that is only beginning to be appreciated.. . .[F]oreign investment continues to be coveted by American leaders who are motivated by the need to create jobs and finance the deficit" (1988:14).

The political pressure was on the Japanese automakers. Unless there were voluntary reductions in imports there would be protectionist legislation to limit imports. Neither of these alternatives was especially attractive to Japanese firms, since it meant a loss of their hard-earned growth in market share and in overall profit margins. It was also clear during this period that the U.S. auto industry had no intention of trying to compete with the Japanese to recapture market share. GM, Chrysler, and Ford were rapidly relocating production facilities outside the United States, hoping that lower wage labor would increase profit margins on the share of the market that they still controlled.

The alternative facing the Japanese automakers was clear, and it had been suggested repeatedly by union officials, corporate executives, and politicians: Produce cars and trucks in the United States!

Thus were born the transplants. Table 1.1 contains basic information on the six Japanese auto assembly plants established in the Midwest corridor in the 1980s. The plants are listed according to the date of start-up of production, with the oldest plant, Honda, at the top of the table. Several important patterns can be observed in this table and warrant further comment.

All of the plants are located in very small communities and in counties of modest population size. The only exception is Mazda, which is located in the small town of Flat Rock but in a county that contains large urban populations in the Detroit-Dearborn areas.

The estimates of company investment at each site are substantial, ranging between $500 million and almost $2 billion. Many plants have plans for expansion that include the addition of engine plants and research facilities.

State investment in acquisition of land, site preparation, road and water improvement, and worker training was also substantial, ranging between $33 million and $150 million. These are conservative estimates, which do not include the cost of interest on bonds or tax abatements. State and local governments also contributed to the incentive package for a transplant, and in some cases federal funds were used to subsidize worker training. Some analysts have indicated that the cost per job of the financial incentive packages was $11,000 in Tennessee, $50,000 in Indiana, and $108,000 in Kentucky. The footnotes to Table 1.1 indicate substantial variation in the estimates of incentives.

The number of employees at the transplants ranges between two and five thousand, with some plants projecting as many as six thousand production workers. Hourly wages for production employees are about $14.00 per hour, which exceeds the wage levels of manufacturing workers in the region. The transplant hourly wage rate is still below the $16.41 wage found in the United States Big Three, which are unionized. Only two of the six transplants—Mazda and Diamond Star—have union representation for production workers.

Production capacity for the transplants varies between 120,000 vehicles and 440,000 vehicles per year. Aggregate production capacity is about 2 million vehicles, which is about the number of cars imported from Japan in 1980.

With the exception of Wayne County, Michigan, the percentages of the

Table 1.1. Characteristics of Transplants

Plant	Location (city and county)	City and county size (1986)	% White (county, 1986)	Site selection date	Start-up date	Company investment	State investment	Employees	Hourly wages (1990)[a]	Union	Projected capacity (cars/year)
Honda	Marysville, OH	8,310		1/80	11/82	$1.3 billion	$21 million[b]	5,300	$14.55	No[i]	360,000
	Union County	31,100	96.3								
	East Liberty, OH (second plant)	1,200		9/87	12/89	$410 million	$67 million[c]	1,800		No	150,000
	Logan County	40,200	97.9								
Nissan	Smyrna, TN	13,610		10/80	6/83	$760 million	$33 million[d]	1,736 (1983)	$13.95	No[i]	440,000 (cars & trucks)
	Rutherford County	102,700	89.5					3,000 (1985)			139,800 (trucks, 1990)
	Expansion				1992	$490 million		4,300 (1992) 6,000 (projected)			95,844 (cars, 1990)
Mazda	Flat Rock, MI	6,570		11/84	9/87	$750 million	$49 million[e]	3,500	$15.13	Yes	240,000
	Wayne County	2,164,300	61.1								
Diamond-Star	Bloomington-Normal, IL	83,140		10/85	4/88	$500–700 million	$83 million[f]	3,100 (1992)		Yes	240,000
	McLean County	122,700	95.0								

Toyota	Georgetown, KY Scott County	12,360 22,200	92.9	12/85	5/88	$800 million (original facility) $300 million (power train plant) $800 million (expansion plant)	$150 million[g]	4,000 (1991) 5,000 (with expansion)	$14.23	No	200,000 (original) 200,000 (expansion) 400,000 (total)
Subaru-Isuzu	Lafayette, IN Tippecanoe County	65,350 124,400	96.6	12/86	9/89	$500 million	$86 million[h]	1,900 (1992)	$13.94	No	120,000 (phase I)

Source: Milward and Newman (1989); Florida and Kenney (1991); City and County Data Book; personal communications with state economic development officials

a The average hourly wage of production workers at General Motors, Ford, and Chrysler was $16.41 in 1990.

b Specific data on Ohio's first incentive package are difficult to obtain.

c $54 million, road access; $11 million, site improvements for water and sewer lines, $2.1 million, worker training. The state sold Honda the Ohio Transportation Research Center for $31 million. Of that, $5.5 million would pay off bonds that were sold to finance the center; $15.5 million would be to repair state highways and county roads that serve the center; $6 million would be for a trust fund administered by Ohio State University to conduct research.

d $22 million, road access; $11 million, worker training. Tolchin and Tolchin (1988) estimate incentives to be $66 million.

e $19 million, worker training (based on Milward and Newman [1989]; Department of Commerce reports $40 million; $5 million, road improvement; $3 million, site rail improvement; $21 million, economic development loan grant (to be recaptured); $15 million, water system improvement; 100% tax abatement for 14 years. Fucini and Fucini (1990) estimate Michigan incentives at $125 million, which includes property tax abatement.

f $28 million, road improvement; $7.5 million, site acquisition; $7 million, water system improvement; $40 million, worker training. Tolchin and Tolchin (1988) estimate incentives to be $118 million.

g $12.5 million, land purchase; $20 million, site preparation; $47 million, road improvements; $65 million, worker training; $5.2 million, Toyota families' education. Gelsanliter (1992) estimates Tennessee incentives at $350 million, which includes the cost of bond interest payments.

h $37 million, road and sewer improvements; $29 million, worker training; $19 million, land acquisition and development; $1 million, transition for Japanese families. Tax abatements, credits, and utility rate reduction are estimated to cost the state another $260 million.

i During the spring and summer of 1985 the UAW obtained signed cards favoring union representation. The UAW claimed that a majority of Honda workers had signed cards and called on Honda to let the union in without an election. Honda refused, claiming that their survey of workers showed that over 70% were opposed to letting the union in without an election. An election was scheduled for December 16, 1985, but three days before the election the UAW filed unfair labor practices charges with the National Labor Relations Board and cancelled the election (Gelsanliter 1992:105).

j On July 27, 1988, a vote on a UAW organizing drive led to a defeat of the union effort. The company had won with about 70% of the vote, 1622 to 718.

nonwhite populations in the sites of the transplants are below the national average. Transplants have been charged with avoiding employment of African-Americans. Honda, for example, restricted job applications to persons living within a thirty-mile radius of Marysville, Ohio, thereby excluding nonwhite residents of Columbus, a city with a large black population (Berggren et al. 1991:15).

Adding to the importance of these major auto assembly plants in their respective locations is the large number of auto parts suppliers that have located in the same general area. Japanese automakers' preference for close and long-term relationships with suppliers is often described as a *just-in-time* system. This arrangement allows transplants to obtain needed parts from between two and eight hours of transit time (Florida and Kenney 1991). This reduces the need for costly stockpiling of parts and the construction of expensive storage facilities. It also facilitates close face-to-face relationships between transplants and suppliers, and relations of trust that contribute to better understanding between customers and suppliers.

It has been suggested that the emerging relationships between transplants and suppliers resemble the *keiretsu* system that is followed in Japan. *Keiretsu* refers to an economic or corporate group composed of a dozen companies that are linked in horizontal (i.e., independent) or vertical (i.e., dominated by a principal company) relationships. The *keiretsu* can include manufacturers, banks, distributors, and export firms embracing diverse sectors of the economy, or they may be a group of companies in a single sector, such as automotives (Rapoport 1991; Mid-America Project, Inc., 1991).

Estimates of the number of auto supplier companies located in the same areas as the transplants vary, and the number appears to be growing as new suppliers come to the United States. Clearly, U.S. supplier firms already existed in the six states under study, and they were concerned primarily with supplying the U.S. auto firms. With the arrival of the transplants, attention has turned to wholly owned or joint-venture Japanese suppliers that have followed the transplants. In 1988, it was estimated that there were 102 Japanese-owned suppliers and 41 Japanese-United States joint venture suppliers in the six Midwest corridor states (Florida, Kenney, and Mair 1988). By 1991, the estimate of Japanese suppliers had grown to 270 (Florida and Kenney 1991). This estimate was for the United States as a whole, but they are believed to be concentrated primarily in the Midwest (the exception being California where the GM-Toyota joint venture NUMMI assembly plant is located).

The combination of the six large auto assembly plants and the hundreds of smaller supplier plants indicates that we are dealing with a new *production network* that is located in the Midwest corridor. The importance of that network for the economic, political, and social life of the region is only beginning to be assessed.

QUESTIONS ABOUT THE TRANSPLANTS

A number of important sociological questions about the transplants provide the focus for this book.

Why Did the Transplants Locate in Six Contiguous States in the Midwest Corridor? The most apparent similarities of the plant locations are their placement in semirural areas with few minorities and access to a younger work force with limited exposure to unions. Each state selected for a transplant also provided an attractive package of tax abatements, land, job training, and low-cost loans. In addition, states were able to attract transplants because of the availability of a skilled labor force, manufacturing infrastructure, favorable business climate, and other quality-of-life amenities.

But surely there were other states that offered competitive incentive packages, and other states that had attractive infrastructure, labor force, and related incentives. Economic geographers have had a long-standing interest in understanding how firms make their location decisions. For example, Milward and Newman (1989) identify the possible determinants of the location decisions of six auto transplants (including five of the six examined in this book, and the GM Saturn plant in Tennessee). They note the importance of transportation and market proximity, which are two of the traditional factors identified by location theory as determinants of location decisions, and the less precise factor of business climate, which is a mix of such things as worker attitudes toward unions, work ethic, and a cooperative political system.

Without denying the significance of such traditional influences on location decisions, it is important to try to take into account the local state in its new role as entrepreneur, actively engaged in attracting new business and offering a number of new incentives to business. For example, Leicht and Jenkens (1991) looked at how variations in the availability of state-level economic development policies (e.g., venture capital funds) are shaped by economic and political structures that can either facilitate or inhibit such policies. Similarly, Grant (1992) examined how state-level business investment from 1970 to 1985 was influenced by a state's business incentive policies, the existence of a fiscal crisis, and the degree of conflict between labor and capital.

The addition of these nonproduction influences to location theory's emphasis on transportation, markets, and infrastructure will permit an assessment of competing views of why the transplants located in the Midwest corridor (Perrucci 1989). One view can be called an *organizational model* and it is most consistent with location theory. It emphasizes the resources that a firm needs to produce at a competitive price. Thus, it will look for things that reduce the cost of production and distribution of products. A second view is the *state model* which emphasizes the political and administrative capacities of the state to deliver credible *long-term* support to foreign transplants. Thus, transplants select a state for location because they are attracted by the activism and commitment of political leaders and the degree of support that these leaders have for their programs. The final view is the *class model*, which assumes that conflict between labor and management is endemic to the structure of capitalism. As a result, location decisions will be greatly influenced by the degree of union and working-class strength that will confront management.

We intend to examine the importance of these three different clusters of factors for answers to the question of why the Midwest corridor was selected as the home for the transplants. Chapter 3 will focus on this topic.

How Is the State's Economic Incentive Package Presented to Various Interest Groups and the Public? Despite all of the discussion in the previous section about wanting to know the reasons for the location choices of the transplants, it is clear that the entire selection process is shrouded in secrecy. Japanese auto company executives do not wish their competitors to know where they are thinking of locating, for that might provide clues about the relative importance of transportation, labor costs, or marketing strategies (Fox 1990). Site selection teams from the auto companies insist that state and local public officials in states under consideration keep their meetings as confidential and low profile as possible (Dirks 1992). Public officials involved in such negotiations report on the difficulties they experienced in trying to honor the auto companies' desire for secrecy and their own open-meeting policies, which would put their negotiations in the public record.

Elected officials at the state and local levels must consider their efforts to attract transplants within the more general framework of the *politics of growth*. Officials are the focus of competing political, business, labor, and environmental interests, and it is expected that such interests would have different positions on a plan to spend tens of millions of dollars of public money to attract a foreign auto plant (Perrucci and Patel 1990). Political power must be exercised to accommodate the competing interest groups and to gain broader public acceptance of a proposed incentive plan that has been negotiated without much public discussion. State and local officials in the six states with transplants can expect to confront a variety of issues raised about the incentive package and the new "corporate citizen" in the community. These issues are listed below and are examined in depth in Chapter 4.

Are Incentives Legal? Is it legal to provide public funds to private corporations and for the state to exercise its right to acquire land from citizens who do not wish to sell it to be used for a private purpose? The state may spend tax money and acquire land for a park or school, but can it do that for a private company?

Are States Giving Too Much? The dollar size of the incentive packages provided to the transplants in some cases averages out to about forty thousand dollars for each new job. Some members of the community may question the wisdom of such actions. Members of the local business community who are often long-standing residents and head family-owned businesses may want to know why they cannot get state assistance to help them compete. Will the state ever get back the money it invested?

Union or Nonunion? Organized labor will be concerned with the actions of transplants that will affect existing unionized labor and the opportunities to unionize production workers after start-up. Members of construction-related unions will want to participate in the construction phase of the transplant project, which will involve several years of work, and they will try to play a role in the selection of workers. Thus, the competing interests of construction firms for nonunion workers and construction unions seeking jobs for their members will have to be negotiated so that the project may proceed without conflict and delay.

What About Quality of Life? Residents in many of the transplant communities face the realities of growth when they think about environmental impacts. The size of the new transplant will spark concern about air and water pollution and the ability of the transplant to comply with existing state and local regulations on emissions of dangerous materials into the air and water. There will also be concern about population growth and its impact on transportation, education, housing, fire and police protection, and a variety of community services. Such questions reflect concern about the potential decline in quality of life and increased taxes to meet the demand for services. How will the state and local governments deal with these concerns from environmental and related groups?

Several books dealing with these issues have appeared recently. Wallace and Rothschild's (1988) book contains a dozen papers that examine the impact of deindustrialization on local and regional social and economic structures. The unifying perspective of the chapters is that the changing global economy is producing long-term structural change in employment, occupational structure, inequality patterns, and urban change. Yanarella and Green (1990) focus their edited volume on the recruitment of the Japanese auto assembly plants in six mid-American states. Several chapters focus on the use of state incentives from an historical and comparative perspective, on the significance of incentives for location decisions, and on the legal issues involved in the use of public funds for private-sector projects. Other chapters are devoted to issues related to specific plants and specific states, with a focus on both public and behind-the-scenes negotiations and conflicts involved in the dynamics of industrial recruiting.

Our third topic involves examination of new managerial strategies for selecting workers and organizing work in the auto transplants.

How Will U.S. Workers Respond to New Approaches to Developing Worker Commitment and to New Strategies to Change the Organization of Work at the Point of Production? The history of managerial strategies directed at workers is a history of efforts to penetrate worker culture and to harness the potential to work and convert it into actual work. The earliest most systematic effort to harness the potential to work is found in the turn-of-the-century program of *scientific management* developed by Frederick W. Taylor, and often referred to as Taylorism. Since that time one can identify numerous theories, programs, and approaches designed to get workers to work better, faster, and happier. The so-called Japanese style of management is but the latest addition to this list and, as with most new approaches, its alleged accomplishments have been greeted with enthusiasm.

Much has been written about Japanese management principles and their application to U.S. workers and work organization, and there is a great deal of controversy surrounding the topic. Some believe that the high level of commitment and performance of Japanese workers can be attributed to unique aspects of Japan's history and culture, which stress collective identification over individualism (Alston 1989). Some have pointed to the influence of "welfare corporatist" structures in Japanese firms, which simultaneously stress worker participation and employee services, resulting in mutual commitment to shared goals (Lincoln and Kalleberg 1985). And some have pointed to the efforts of the state and corporations in Japan to eliminate national unions, thereby creating a more vulnerable work force less able to resist management programs to increase productivity (Cusumano 1985).

The most sharply contrasting views on Japanese production methods are provided by a research group with the International Motor Vehicle Program at the Massachusetts Institute of Technology (MIT), and another group from the Royal Institute of Technology in Stockholm. Womack, Jones, and Roos (1990) from MIT view Japanese style *lean production* (also called Toyotism) as a model of an innovative and productive system that produces high-quality products with a dedicated work force. It is called *lean* because it "uses less of everything compared with mass production— half the human effort in the factory, half the manufacturing space, half the investment in tools, half the engineering hours to develop a new product in half the time" (p. 13). Workers under lean production will be expected to broaden their skills to carry out many different jobs as contributing members of a team, in contrast to the narrow specialization of tasks and hundreds of different job titles found in the U.S. auto industry's mass production methods.

Berggren (1992), from the Swedish research group, acknowledges some of the positive features of lean production but is most critical of the intensity of work, the expansion of work time, and the potential for work-related injuries. He claims that the MIT group provides little evidence of how workers respond to working conditions under Japanese-style management, and is skeptical of the claims of greater productivity under lean production (Berggren, Bjorkman, and Hollander 1991). In general, Berggren sees greater continuity between Toyotism (lean production) and Taylorism (mass production) in that the work is still highly standardized, the so-called multiskilled worker is really doing small variations on the same job, and worker self-management really means participation in rationalizing your own work.

We know from several case studies that Japanese auto assembly plants devote considerable time and effort to the selection and training of production employees (generally referred to as associates; Hill, Indegaard, and Fujita 1989; Fucini and Fucini 1990; Graham 1991). In the case of Mazda (a unionized plant) there was a five-step evaluation process:

1. written tests on mechanical, verbal, and writing skills,
2. interviews devoted to work experience and seeing "if the individual can survive in the Mazda environment" (Hill et al. 1989:79)
3. real-life simulations to see how applicants deal with interpersonal problems,
4. a medical exam, and
5. an actual job simulation to evaluate an applicant's ability to handle the physical demands of the job.

The six-month testing and evaluation process is followed by a three-month training program for the successful recruit (Hill et al. 1989).

Graham's (1991) participant-observer study of Subaru-Isuzu (SIA), a nonunion transplant, reveals a similar lengthy process of selection and training. Her study also provides rich detail of how the applicants and recruits respond to the rigorous selection process. SIA selected its 1,700 workers from 30,000 applicants, and Mazda had 96,500 applicants from which to select 3,500 workers. The large number of applicants enables the transplants to select a younger work force (and hence less likely to incur health costs) that is indifferent or hostile to unions and receptive to Japanese style of work organization and management. Fucini and Fucini (1990) describe Mazda's approach as an attempt to build a *third culture*, combining Japanese team concepts with American temperament without changing the basic management principles. As they put it: "The third-culture plant would be American in its external appearance, but its substance would always be Japanese" (p. 44).

Drawing on survey data from 6 Japanese auto assembly transplants and 73 Japanese auto supplier plants, Florida and Kenney report that "both transplant assemblers and suppliers have been remarkably successful in implanting the Japanese system of work organization in the U.S. environment" (1991:391). The interpretation of this high degree of success emphasizes the effectiveness of work force selection and socialization. However, field research in a transplant raises questions about the extent to which the Japanese system has been embraced on the shop floor (Graham 1991). Despite the emphasis on work teams, cooperation, and worker participation in decision-making, the demands of day-to-day work bring issues of speed-up, safety, and arbitrary authority to the forefront of labor-management relations (Fucini and Fucini 1990).

It is too soon to conclude that the Japanese approach to organizing work is an unqualified success, and that American workers have accepted the cooperative style as an alternative to the adversarial style of organized labor. We examine such issues in greater depth in Chapter 5.

The fourth and final topic examined in this book is concerned with the future.

What Will Be the Long-Term Impact of the Auto Transplants on Local and Regional Social and Economic Structures?   Political and business elites who have developed and supported the state's economic incentive package expect long-term gains to the community because of expanded employment in the transplants and auto supplier plants, and secondary employment. Other projections of economic costs and negative quality of life consequences point to the need for additional basic services like police and fire protection, sewer systems, and road maintenance. A growing population will also require greater expenditures for housing, education, and recreational facilities (Koebel 1987). What do we expect will be the net balance of positive and negative consequences of the transplants?

Preliminary evidence from research conducted in two transplant communities indicates a mixture of positive and negative outcomes and a balance of public perceptions about benefits and costs. Wenum and Chapman's (1992) research in Bloomington-Normal, Illinois, provides a very positive assessment of the economic impact of the Diamond-Star plant. They project that by 1998 nearly two-thirds of the state and local expenses for Diamond-Star will be paid off by the plant's property tax revenue, and income and sales taxes by employees. These estimates do not include property taxes paid by auto supplier plants in the area or the income and sales taxes paid by their employees. Wenum and Chapman also report that the growth that followed Diamond-Star has not drastically changed the areas of housing, social welfare, and school enrollments. These smaller than anticipated impacts may be due to the relatively large size of the two cities and county (see Table 1.1), which makes it easier to absorb a growing population.

Houghland (1991) conducted telephone interviews with central Kentucky residents each year between 1986 and 1990 concerning their view of the Toyota plant and its place in their community. The public's views of Toyota's role in the community is extremely positive, and notes Toyota's support for the community and its employees. However, there are still a sizable number of Kentuckians (about 30 percent) who have not made up their minds about whether Toyota "takes care of its employees," "works its employees too hard," "rewards loyalty and teamwork," and "is a good place to work."

The ambivalence about Toyota's image as a corporate citizen and employer is also reflected in responses to other questions. Central Kentuckians believe overwhelmingly that the plant is benefiting their community and its residents, especially in terms of jobs, wages, and business activity. However, they also overwhelmingly perceive increased traffic congestion, more pollution, crowded schools, and higher housing costs. This seems to suggest regret about the loss of the benefits of small town life, but a realization that these losses must be balanced against the benefits of growth. The views of Kentuckians about Toyota as an employer and corporate citizen will undoubtedly change as relationships develop in their new partnership of capital and community.

What about the broader impact of the transplants on the U.S. auto industry in the region and across the country? Scholars differ in their views of the benefits of the transplants and the free-market mechanisms that facilitate their location in the Midwest corridor. Reich (1990) has a positive view of the transplants, emphasizing the new job creation, the money invested in upgrading skills of U.S. workers, and the transfer of new manufacturing technology, which will contribute to productivity and U.S. competitiveness in the world economy. Moreover, Reich is opposed to efforts that might limit investment in the United States by foreign corporations. In contrast, Howes (1991a) has called for the regulation of foreign investment, emphasizing how auto transplants have had a negative impact on the U.S. auto industry and parts makers. Howes believes that the transplants and foreign auto suppliers will eliminate more jobs in the United States than they will create.

It will take some time before future research can assess the impact of the transplants on the communities and regions in which they are located, and on the U.S. auto industry. Chapters 6 and 7 look at some of the long-term consequences of the transplants.

THEORY APPLIED TO THE TRANSPLANTS:
EMBEDDED CORPORATISM

We approach the four topics discussed above, and the more general situation of Japanese auto transplants in the Midwest corridor, with reference to two concepts: corporatism and embeddedness. We combine these concepts in a way that helps us to understand what is happening in the six states that are home to the auto transplants.

Corporatism is a political theory that is derived from a western European experience, and is offered as an alternative to pluralism and to the industrial conflict and competition endemic to capitalism. As Schmitter states, it is an "institutional arrangement for linking the associationally organized interests of civil society with the decisional structures of the state" (1979:9). In the corporatism model, the organized interests of competitive groups in the economy, such as labor or agriculture, agree to be represented by a peak association (e.g., AFL-CIO, National Association of Manufacturers) and to allow that association to speak for all persons in the sector (Wilson 1982). The government, in consultation with all major interests, makes the major decisions on the economy.

Critics of corporatist theory (Wilson 1982; Salisbury 1979) and its applicability to the United States have pointed to the diversity and fragmentation of interests on the national level. Growing interest diversity and differentiation of functions in advanced societies appears to limit the emergence of powerful peak associations. As Salisbury notes, "the only way for a corporatist system to develop would be for the would-be peak associations to achieve hegemonic status through their own organizational processes" (1979:223).

A number of analysts have recognized the limitations of the corporatism concept for the United States as a national system, and have shifted attention to regional or sectorial corporatism, or to mesocorporatism (Cawson 1985; Cowan and Buttel 1988; Gray and Lowery 1990; Young 1990). These formulations emphasize the role of state mediation between two antagonistic forces, seeking to shape a new partnership by incorporating them into the policymaking process.

Many of the formulations of corporatism in its classic European form or modified U.S. version appear to stress overorganized conceptions of the linkages, relationships, and binding authority in the system. This overemphasis on the formal-legal properties of corporatism underplays the role of informal patterns of ties and influence between agencies of the state and corporations that can effectively shape policy. Our effort to retain the concept of corporatism for the analysis of economic action in the Midwest corridor points to the role of the local state as an activist and autonomous actor in economic policymaking that impacts local economies. The local state has taken the lead in providing venture capital funds, stimulating technological innovation, redirecting public education, restructuring labor-management relations, and bringing higher education into new partnerships with private corporations (Osborne 1988).

Embeddedness is a perspective on economic behavior put forward by Granovetter to counteract the emphasis of neoclassical economics on "rational, self-interested behavior affected minimally by social relations" (1985:481). The perspective locates purposive economic action in ongoing systems of social relations, pointing to the interweaving of business relations and sociability that contribute to the development of trust and order in economic life. Coleman has described Granovetter's approach as

> an attempt to introduce into the analyses of economic systems social and organizational relations, not merely as a structure that springs into place to fulfill an economic function, but as a structure with history and continuity that give it an independent impact on the functioning of the system. (1990:302)

In our view, embedded corporatism involves

1. an activist local state working with segments of the business class (the "growth coalition," as discussed by Molotch [1976]) to develop an industrial policy that fosters technological advances and confronts the challenge of global competition
2. an ideology expressing a new partnership of business, labor, and government to advance common interests in economic growth,
3. the penetration of the structure and ideology of corporatism into a variety of elite networks, and
4. the ability to penetrate and mobilize noneconomic interest groups to provide indirect or tacit endorsement of the corporatist project or its ideology.

Our formulation of embedded corporatism has an obvious resemblance to the idea of the "growth machine" as developed by Molotch (1976) and Logan and Molotch (1987). They point to the importance of growth as an overriding goal of local elites, the belief that "growth makes jobs" as the ideological support for growth projects, and the role of noneconomic associations (e.g., public schools, athletic events) that support growth through local boosterism. However, there are several important differences. In the growth machine, competing land interest groups at the local level attempt to seek action at the state government level that will enhance the growth potential of the local area. In short, the local growth coalition is the initiator of action that will benefit land-based interests. In corporatism, it is state government that initiates new economic policies and the ideology of a new partnership that will impact on local communities. The local growth coalition is active to the extent of trying to make its community the most attractive site for a project that is being negotiated by the state government and a foreign corporation.

A second difference concerns how the politics of growth is conducted. In the growth machine, the "politics of distribution" (i.e., who gets the goods and services in the community) is hidden from public view, "largely unseen, and relegated to negotiations within committees" (Molotch 1976:313). In corporatism, the project being negotiated between the state and the foreign corporation takes place in public view, with detailed descriptions of the state's incentive package in the state legislature and local newspapers. In fact, as we shall discuss below, the public debate over the incentive package is a matter of critical importance to the foreign investor.

The final difference concerns the role played by noneconomic groups in supporting local growth projects. In the growth machine formulation, *auxiliary players* (e.g., museums, theaters, universities, symphonies, and professional sports teams) are involved in promoting and maintaining growth (Logan and Molotch 1987:75). Auxiliary players have a smaller stake in growth than the land-based elite and politicians, but their institutions depend on support from the growth coalition. In our use of the concept of embeddedness, we stress a different type of participation by auxiliary players. They are not called upon to support community growth in general or specific growth projects—for these are economic objectives— but simply to carry out their educational, cultural, or humanitarian activities in a manner that indirectly and tacitly supports the corporatist project. Our concept of embeddedness is more subtle than the boosterism of the auxiliary players in the growth machine, and stresses the construction of a network of supportive social relationships between groups with economic and noneconomic interests.

The concept of embedded corporatism allows us to understand how the changing global economy has resulted in different patterns of economic development across countries and regions within countries. A six-state region in the United States, referred to as the Midwest corridor, has been the location for six Japanese auto transplants. The transplants are represented as a new form of public-private cooperation for economic development, and a new way of organizing work in the automobile industry.

Corporatism involves an activist local state working with the business class to attract foreign investment and thereby stimulate the local economy. This goal is pursued within the framework of a corporatist ideology that speaks of a new partnership between government, business, labor, and universities (with the two latter being very passive or marginal to the partnership) that serves the interests of most segments of the community.

We have suggested that in order for this form of local corporatism to work, it must become embedded within the institutional structure of the local community. The process of embeddedness is facilitated by the politics of the incentive package, the selection and training of production workers, media coverage of the transplant, and the personal and organizational ties established with noneconomic segments of the community. If we could describe the process colloquially, we might say that corporatism brought transplants to the heart of the country, but embeddedness put the transplants in the heart of the heart of the country.

It should also be noted that our discussion of embedded corporatism is not limited to the relation between a transplant, the local state, and the local community. Although neglected in our analysis, there is the larger fact that the transplants in each state are part of a larger production system of foreign firms that work with the transplant in the manufacture and marketing of products. These firms are located throughout the six-state region as part of just-in-time production that is typically followed in the transplants. Many of these supplier firms may also have received incentives from the state or local community, thereby reproducing the process described above for the transplant. In addition, the political and economic interests that brought suppliers to the state would also be involved in creating a favorable climate for the new firm by enlisting the support of local civic, religious, educational, and cultural groups.

Thus, the activities of the transplants, and the political-business elites who support them, must be extended to incorporate the hundreds of Japanese-owned transplant suppliers and Japan-United States joint venture suppliers that are located in the Midwest corridor (Florida et al. 1988:9). The entire production system of the transplants can extend the impact of corporatism far beyond the communities in which the transplants are located. It is too soon to know if the situation in the Midwest corridor will remain at its present level of simply providing initiatives to attract transplants, or if it is the beginning of an evolving business-government-community relationship that will be concerned with commu-

nity infrastructure and a broader set of needs of transplant employees
and local residents.

In the next chapter we examine the historical context for the transplant
phenomenon. We consider the economic and political forces released by a
changing global economy, and how these forces affected states and communities in the United States. It is out of this context that the corporatist
project that is embodied in the transplants took root in the Midwest
corridor.

Chapter 2

The Global-Local Connection: How the Changing Global Economy Affected States and Communities

A world economy that exceeds the political grasp of modern nation-states is a reality that produces domestic economic restructuring and threatens worker welfare and community stability
—Gene F. Summers, "Preface to Deindustrialization: Restructuring the Economy"

The coming of the Japanese auto transplants to the United States in the 1980s was but one consequence of major changes that were taking place in the world economy. The once stable patterns of investment, production, and employment within particular countries were shattered, with little regard for national boundaries that once defined where steel was produced or where cars were made. The rapid movement of investment capital, the flexibility of production systems, and the interchangeability of international labor made it possible for new industries to arise in the most unlikely locations and for once mighty industrial giants to be humbled.

HISTORICAL CONTEXT FOR THE TRANSPLANT PHENOMENON

For nearly thirty years following World War II the United States dominated the global economy, accounting for three-fourths of the world's invested capital and two-thirds of its industrial capacity. As a consequence, by 1950 the gross national product (GNP) of the United States was three times that of the Soviet Union, nine times that of Germany, and twelve times that of Japan. During this period there were sharp increases in the dollar value of U.S. exports, foreign investment, and overseas bank assets. In addition to the extensive investment by private sector corporations and financial institutions, the geopolitical actions of the United States aimed at containing and isolating the Soviet Union resulted in billions of dollars of foreign aid to Western European and Asian countries that would soon become competitors. The Soviet Union and its East European allies also embarked on long term programs to rebuild their industrial plants and strengthen their economies.

By the mid-1970s, the steady improvements in the war-torn economies of many nations produced important shifts in the balance of economic power among industrialized nations. The U.S. (GNP) was now less than twice that of the Soviet Union, less than four times that of Germany, and less than three times that of Japan. With more new players in the global economy, the U.S. rate of economic growth slowed. Between 1970 and 1978 the GNP in the United States grew by 129 percent, compared to 137 percent in the Soviet Union, 152 percent in Japan, 170 percent in China, 135 percent in France, and 153 percent in Poland. Although these relative gains in GNP reflect the gigantic size of the U.S. economy and the lower starting point and therefore greater growth potential of the other countries, there were also signs of significant weakening of the U.S. economy in several basic sectors. The United States' share of world production in steel, coal, oil, and autos declined between 1950 and the late 1970s, and profits from the domestic economy declined sharply between the mid-1960s and mid-1970s.

Many of these changes in the position of the United States in the world economy could be viewed as the normal workings of a healthy national and global economy that shifts temporary advantage to different industries and countries. For example, the decline in position of the United States relative to other countries in the mid-1970s could be attributed to a number of temporary conditions that could easily be corrected.

First, the success of U.S. firms in their direct and indirect investments in foreign countries resulted in the creation of multinational subsidiaries that acquired the technical-managerial knowledge necessary for creating competitive firms. The growth of competition within certain industries might limit the profits of U.S. firms, but the advantage of size, productivity, and technical know-how should return the United States to its position of dominance.

The loss of competitive advantage in the auto and steel industries was due to the failure of top management in U.S. firms to respond to foreign competition in the traditional and accepted way of seeking new markets, investing in research and development, and developing more efficient technology. They underestimated the impact of rising oil prices on consumer demand for more fuel-efficient cars that were smaller and lighter because of lower steel content.

Third, the strength of organized labor resulted in increased labor costs that made U.S. products less competitive. Cost-of-living wage contracts, increased job security, and union control over work rules increased the cost of labor without offsetting gains in productivity.

A final reason for loss of profits and market share is that the federal government imposed a wide array of regulations on U.S. firms, which increased the cost of doing business. Meeting standards of the Occupational Safety and Health Administration (OSHA) and the Environmental Protection Agency (EPA), for example, placed exceptional burdens on American business at a time when international competition was on the upswing.

If any or all of the above factors had been the only things involved in the declining position of the United States in the global economy it might have been possible for the United States to reestablish its dominance in the world economy. But something else was going on that would make it difficult for the U.S. economy to bounce back and reestablish the old equilibrium.

Between the mid-1960s and the mid-1970s, corporate profits from the domestic economy across twelve industries declined by 46 percent. In the early 1960s the annual rate of return on investment was 15.5 percent. In the late 1960s it was 12.7 percent. In the early 1970s it was about 10 percent, and after 1975 it never rose above 10 percent again. During this same period, U.S. investment abroad showed continued growth, and the share of corporate profits from foreign investments increased steadily (Bluestone and Harrison 1982).

In an effort to reestablish higher profit margins, major corporations had begun to shift capital investments to different regions within the United States and to overseas operations. The resulting capital flight to low-wage areas and corporate downsizing eliminated over 11 million jobs between 1979 and 1984 due to plant shutdowns, relocations, and layoffs (Office of Technology Assessment, OTA, 1986). In the same time period, the OTA study reported that some 8 million new jobs were created, 94 percent of which were in the service sector. However, in contrast to the manufacturing jobs that were permanently lost in traditional smokestack industries, service workers were employed for fewer hours per week and at lower hourly wages (Harrison and Bluestone 1988).

Public response to this massive job loss was muted because of the belief that the major unemployment was concentrated in the so called Rust Belt—the northeast and midwestern states with large manufacturing sectors. In actuality, the problem was national in scope, with some of the hardest hit regions in the Sun Belt, despite the belief that they were experiencing growth and prosperity (Wallace and Rothschild 1988).

The rate of growth of new jobs also led many to believe that displaced workers would quickly be reabsorbed into an expanding economy. For example, in Indiana there was a loss of 11,500 jobs in manufacturing between October 1985 and October 1986, and there was an increase of 35,000 jobs in retail trade. This appears to be an important gain in total employees and would make one discount the job loss that was occurring. However, a closer look at these figures indicates that almost all of the 11,500 jobs that were lost (10,000 to be exact) were in the steel mills, where workers' average pay was $11.11 per hour and average work week hours was 41.2 hours. In contrast, the 35,000 new retail workers averaged $5.86 per hour for a 29.5 hour average work week. Thus, the large net gain in number of employees resulted in a net loss in gross earnings. This same pattern holds for all manufacturing jobs lost and gained in Indiana in the 1985–1986 period. The gain in low-wage jobs obscured the loss of high-wage jobs and the consequent loss of revenue to the state's economy.

Harrison and Bluestone (1988) examine national data on wages and family income, which indicate a steady deterioration in the economic opportunities of most Americans. Beginning about 1973, real average weekly earnings (adjusted for inflation) began a long-term decline that continues today, and "median annual family income stopped growing, even though more family members were working than ever before" (p. 5). And while the job growth of the 1980s produced some high-paying jobs, the proportion of full-time workers earning low wages increased steadily from 1979 onward. The restructuring of the economy, with its plant closings and downsizing, was eliminating millions of middle-income jobs in manufacturing and creating low-wage replacements.

A recognition of this situation has even reached the highest levels of government for the first time in over a decade. Secretary of Labor Robert B. Reich, writing in the *New York Times*, has acknowledged the growing inequality that has resulted from the trade-off of good jobs for more jobs:

> Our bigger long-term problem is creating jobs that pay well. The average wages of America's production workers, adjusted for inflation, are the lowest they've been since 1967. Eighteen percent of full-time workers don't earn enough to keep a family of four out of poverty; the level is up from 12 percent in 1979. And more Americans who want full-time jobs are working part-time instead. (Reich 1993:A15)

Thus, capital flight and disinvestment introduced major changes in the U.S. economy and its occupational structure. Industrial sectors that had once been dominated by U.S. firms, such as auto, steel, and rubber, gave

way to reduced market share and increased competition from international corporations.

The process of deindustrialization and permanent job loss due to restructuring of the economy accelerated the decline of union strength in
the United States, a traditional source of support for high wages and job
security. From a high point of 35 percent of the labor force unionized in
the mid-1950s, today the figure is below 20 percent, and only 12 percent in
the private sector. As a result of actual and threatened plant closures and
relocations, workers were vulnerable to a variety of corporate strategies
aimed at reducing wages, benefits, and union representation. Results of
National Labor Relations Board (NLRB) elections for union representation between 1955 and 1980 indicate increasing difficulty of winning such
elections and a decline in the size of the potential bargaining unit involved in certification elections (Wallace and Rothschild 1988). The actions of organized capital to gain advantage in its struggle with labor are
consistent with the long history of capital-labor conflict (Griffin, Wallace,
and Rubin 1986). By the mid-1980s the changing global economy and the
mobility of capital in pursuit of more favorable investment opportunities
gave corporations the upper hand in their efforts to exercise control over
the labor process. What was unknown, however, was how this opportunity to control would be developed and applied.

Along with deindustrialization and rising unemployment in the 1970s
came an unprecedented series of annual trade deficits. In the early 1960s,
imports of foreign products played a small part in the American economy, but by 1980 imports accounted for 22 percent of all goods purchased
by Americans. The significance of foreign competition was described very
pointedly by Reich.

> By 1980 more than 70 percent of all the goods produced in the United
> States were actively competing with foreign made goods. . . .Beginning in
> the mid-1960's, foreign imports have claimed an increasing share of the
> American market. By 1981 America was importing almost 26 percent of its
> cars, 25 percent of its steel, 60 percent of its televisions, radios, tape re-
> corders, and phonographs, 43 percent of its calculators, 27 percent of its
> metal-forming machine tools, 35 percent of its textile machinery, and 53
> percent of its numerically controlled machine tools. Twenty years before,
> imports had accounted for less than 10 percent of the U.S. market for each of
> these products. Between 1970 and 1980 imports from developing nations
> increased almost tenfold, from $3.6 billion to $30 billion (in constant dollars).
> (1983:121–22)

Glickman and Woodward (1989:Chapter 4) describe how concern over
the mounting trade deficit led the Reagan administration to follow a
policy to allow the U.S. dollar to decline against the Japanese yen, Ger-

man mark, and British pound: "The cheaper dollar was the last hope to improve the American trade balance by making our goods less expensive when sold abroad and to make foreign goods more expensive here" (p. 114). What was not anticipated was that foreigners would take the abundance of dollars they had been accumulating from trade surpluses and buy American real estate and companies. Thus, the U.S. dollar policy attracted foreign direct investment, and "provided one additional bonus: it reduced production costs vis-à-vis other nations" (p. 116). Such conditions would be very attractive to Japanese auto companies thinking of building plants in the United States.

The intersection of structural change in the U.S. economy, plant closings, and increased unemployment put heavy pressure on national and state economies. Declining tax revenue led government at all levels to search for ways to reduce spending. At the national level, the combination of increased spending for defense and reduced revenue from the Reagan-inspired tax cuts for upper income groups resulted in federal deficits that demanded cuts in the federal budget. The first target for cuts was federal assistance to the states.

Federal assistance to state and local governments is distributed in three ways. The first and largest category of aid is categorical grants, which provide money for specific purposes, such as job retraining or fighting drug abuse. States and localities are required to spend the money for specific problems and for specific segments of the population. The second way that funds are distributed is through block grants, which provide a sum of money for several programs and the money can be apportioned by local authorities. The third and least used mode of distributing funds is general revenue sharing. Such funds can be used by local authorities with very few federal controls or limitations.

During a twenty-year period beginning in the mid-1950s, federal aid to the states as a percentage of GNP increased from 0.8 to 3.7 percent. As Eisenger reports: "In constant (1972) dollars the amount of assistance in this period rose from $5.6 billion to $49.4 billion, and the number of separate programs soared from 132 in 1960 to 492 in 1978" (1988:67). But beginning in 1978 during the Carter administration there was a steady decline in the flow of dollars from federal to state and local treasuries. The Reagan administration accelerated this decline as it tried to reduce federal spending by cutting the total dollars to states and shifting money out of categorical grants and into block grants. Between 1980 and 1987, federal grants-in-aid to state and local governments shrank by more than 22 percent, or $10.5 billion.

The change in relationship between the federal and state governments associated with the decline in grants-in-aid to states was more important than simply a loss of revenue to states. Rather, states were being asked to take greater responsibility for the welfare of its citizens, and to do it from their own revenue. Unfortunately, all revenue streams to states and localities were down due to deindustrialization, recession, and shrinking federal assistance. But the demand for public services was on the increase, with the business community looking for new ways to stimulate growth and to help existing firms, and with the rising number of unemployed seeking assistance in job retraining and social welfare benefits. There was also the need to maintain the infrastructure of schools, roads, parks, and safety so that communities would remain supportive of existing business residents and attractive to new ones.

The crisis facing many states in the early 1980s has been described very clearly by Ferman (1984) in his analysis of how the recession impacted on the availability of human services in Michigan. In the early 1980s, Michigan had unemployment rates of 12–15 percent a year, which exceeded the national rate by 50–75 percent. Declining tax revenues from the economic downturn coincided with declining federal subsidies at a time when the demand for human services was increasing. The demand for human services from the expanding unemployed population had to compete with other service needs vying for support in the following areas:

> (1) economic development to create new jobs; (2) rebuilding the city infrastructure to repair and maintain roads and buildings; and (3) securing the environment by maintaining adequate protection services (police, fire, sanitation). Since federal and state subsidies for all three have been reduced, we anticipate more and more pressure on human service programs, which will be cut still more in order to fund these other public activities (Ferman 1984:136)

Many states, especially those experiencing deindustrialization, came to share the experience of Michigan. What actions did they take to deal with their fiscal and social crisis? What was the national context for these actions, in terms of the ideological and policy debates that were on the public agenda? How were these debates related to the transplant phenomenon?

RESPONSE TO THE CHANGING GLOBAL ECONOMY

The speed with which the changing global economy was transforming the occupational structure and the spatial distribution of industry and employment across the United States sparked an active debate in political and policy circles. Officials at the highest levels of government in the 1980s remained sanguine about the underlying strength of the economy and its prospects for growth. President Reagan, in a 1985 report to Congress, stated:

> The progression of an economy such as America's from agricultural to manufacturing to services is a natural change.. . .The move from an industrial society toward a post-industrial service economy has been one of the greatest changes to affect the developed world since the Industrial Revolution. (Miller and Castellblanch 1988:6)

Some economic theories provided support for political leaders who viewed deindustrialization as part of the normal workings of an otherwise healthy economy. Drawing upon the views of the late Joseph Schumpeter (1939), who saw economic dislocations such as plant closings as examples of "creative destruction," eliminating inefficient operations and providing new economic opportunities, one could be optimistic about deindustrialization. For example, McKenzie states: "As some firms go under, they release their resources to other, more cost-effective firms that offer consumers more of what they want at more attractive prices" (1984:85).

Optimism is extended not only to a revitalized economy, but also to the displaced workers who may enjoy some new benefits and opportunities. Once again, McKenzie:

> Many people lose their jobs when plants are closed, but their loss does not necessarily mean that they are somehow worse off. Workers unemployed because their plants close are also beneficiaries of the competitive process (involving closings and openings) in other markets which yields higher quality goods at lower prices. Workers unemployed because of their firms' failures can sometimes find other jobs in expanding sectors of the economy—in those firms that are winning the competitive struggle. Furthermore, workers unemployed by plant closings are often compensated in advance for their expected loss in income when their plants close. When the risk of plant closing is high, the supply of labor is often restricted (who would prefer to work where the loss of employment is highly probable or imminent?). As a result, in those risky jobs wages are comparatively high, with the wage differential providing a form of prepaid compensation for the risk of unemployment. (1984:87)

Those who hold more pessimistic views see the economy as permanently deindustrializing and have serious doubts about the health of the U.S. economy without a strong manufacturing sector (Bluestone and Harrison 1982). In 1960, manufacturing employment accounted for 31 percent of the work force, declining to 27.4 percent in 1970, and 19.8 percent in 1983. The loss of such high-wage jobs threatens to undercut the productivity gains that fuel economic growth and to weaken the high-wage service sector jobs that are linked to manufacturing (Miller and Castellblanch 1988; Cohen and Zysman 1987).

There is also reason to be pessimistic about the impact of deindustrialization on the communities that experience plant closings and on the displaced workers who are the casualties of industrial decline (Bluestone and Harrison 1982; Perrucci, Perrucci, Targ, and Targ 1988). Communities are faced with sudden loss of payroll taxes, property taxes, and charitable contributions, bringing economic and social stress far beyond the closed plant. Many displaced workers, rather than being quickly reabsorbed into the economy, remain unemployed for long periods of time. A national survey of 5.1 million displaced workers between 1979 and 1984 reported that the median length of time without work was twenty-four weeks, and that one-fourth of the workers were without work for one year or more (OTA 1986). A case study of a single plant closing found that 71 percent of displaced workers were unemployed eight months after the plant closed (Perrucci et al. 1988). Both national studies and case studies report that reemployed workers experience substantial income loss in their new jobs (Flaim and Sehgal 1985; Ashton and Iadicola 1986).

The impact of deindustrialization on communities and displaced workers is shaped by the health and vitality of national and local economies. Reemployment opportunities are related to the general level of unemployment at the time and to the availability of high-wage jobs. There is some evidence from the study of displaced workers in one state that the reemployment rate of displaced workers is better in an expanding rather than declining local economy. However, the reemployed workers who previously held high-wage jobs ($12 per hour in 1989) experienced a 36 percent cut in wages in new jobs, while those who previously held low-wage jobs ($4.80–5.60 per hour in 1989) experienced a 6–15 percent increase in wages in new jobs (Perrucci, Perrucci, Targ, and Targ 1991). The experience of these reemployed workers indicates that the changing economy has significantly transformed the occupational and wage structures, leaving millions of full-time workers whose wages put them in or at the margins of poverty.

The debate between those who were optimistic about the opportunities associated with a changing global economy and those who saw the United States standing by idly while the nation's industrial strength was eroded had important implications for many governors and state legislatures that were facing serious economic problems. Among the recurring themes in the debate over deindustrialization is the contrast between *market* and *statist* solutions to the challenge of global competition (Reich 1983; Johnson 1982; Katzenstein 1985). Advocates of a market approach generally call for removal of impediments to capital investment, such as environmental regulations and excessive taxes on profits and capital gains, and replacing them with attractive incentives for investment. The role of government is minimal, providing favorable conditions for business and allowing competitive forces of the market to work. One example of this approach is the proposal to create *enterprise zones* in areas with limited economic opportunities. Enterprise zones are areas of high unemployment and low family incomes. The objective is to bring jobs to these areas, and it is achieved by relaxing a variety of federal regulations concerning environmental pollution, occupational health and safety standards, wages, and taxes on profits. Investors who take advantage of these opportunities are expected to hire local residents and thereby contribute to the local economy.

A more statist approach to the problems of deindustrialization is often discussed with reference to the remarkable economic success of the Japanese and their state-guided industrial policy. Advocates of an explicit industrial policy call upon the U.S. government to identify those sectors of the economy that are vital to long-term growth and global competition, and to strengthen them with a variety of policies. For example, if it is decided that the auto industry, steel industry, or semiconductor industry is vital to the overall economy, then we must do what is necessary to maintain it in global competition: by subsidizing research on technologies that will make it more competitive; by funding training programs to create a more skilled and productive work force; by fostering cooperative, joint efforts among private-sector firms to develop new products and protecting such firms against the large financial risks that might follow.

While the debate over deindustrialization was engaging politicians, policy analysts, and academics at the national level, most states were quietly, and with little fanfare, going about the business of coping with deindustrialization and the changing global economy. Robert Goodman (1979) observed this process and provided an instructive account of how states were competing for outside capital, which he referred to as "regional wars." Despite the hyperbole of the military metaphor, there was a sense that something new was at work in efforts by states to ignite their economies. Traditionally, states have competed by calling attention to such things as the availability of land, labor, and transportation, and to the general quality of life in an area that is provided by climate, culture, leisure activities, and the educational system. More recently, there have been additions to these routine incentives, resulting in an expanding list of economic incentives including tax abatements, job training, research incubators, and low-cost loans, sometimes involving hundreds of millions of dollars of public funds.

When Goodman's book appeared, the most prominent case of a state using an economic incentive package to attract a foreign automobile plant involved the Volkswagen plant in East Huntington, Pennsylvania. The state of Pennsylvania provided $71 million in low-interest loans, rail and highway improvements, job recruiting, and tax abatements for a $200 million plant that opened in 1978 and employed about 2,500 workers. (That plant shut down in July 1988.) As scholars turned their attention to these activities by state governments it became clear that the state-as-entrepreneur is not a new role for states, but that the scale and direction of state actions has changed.

State involvement in economic development activities has a long and varied history. Hansen (1990) reports on the activities of states (i.e., colonies) before the American Revolution to promote business, and of continued state involvement in paying for development of canals and railroads throughout the nineteenth century. As the capacity for planning and economic forecasting improved in the early and midtwentieth century, more states became involved in trying to influence economic activity. An in-depth examination of the rise of economic development activism by states is provided by Eisenger (1988), who starts with an examination of the depression era to uncover the roots of economic development policies, and traces the development of the entrepreneurial state in the mid-1980s.

Studies of the level of state activity in fostering economic development indicate that business promotion policies have increased in number and have been widely disseminated across the states. Traditional policies of tax breaks have expanded to include direct expenditure of state funds, venture capital programs, and export promotion programs (Hansen 1990:11). The total number of specific programs in the fifty states almost doubled between 1966 and 1985 (from 840 programs to 1,633 programs), reaching an average of 32 programs per state (Eisenger 1988:19).

But more important than the number of business incentive programs available from state and local governments is the particular type of programs that have developed in recent years. Several analysts have attempted to classify development policies in order to identify the changes that have been occurring. Table 2.1 identifies traditional economic development policies, and so-called new-wave policies. Traditional forms of direct assistance to businesses involve a combination of financial incentives and other state services that would encourage business to locate in an area or to expand its activities. Many of these traditional policies are generalized benefits that are available across most sectors of the business community. Advertising the virtues of a particular location through brochures or participation at trade fairs is of potential benefit to many firms. The same could be said of tax relief programs, worker training, and provision of infrastructure (e.g., water, roads) at plant sites. Traditional policies have a common focus on trying to reduce the cost of doing business and thereby increase profits.

Table 2.1. A Typology of State and Local Economic Development Policies
that Directly Aid Businesses

Traditional Economic Development Policies
(Primarily Targeted at Branch Plant Recruitment)

Marketing Area As Branch Plant Location
  Industrial development advertising
  Marketing trips to corporate headquarters
  Provision of site information to prospects
Financial Incentives
  Industrial revenue bonds
  Property tax abatements
  Other tax relief
  Provision of land at below-market prices
  Direct state loans
Nonfinancial Incentives to Branch Plants
  Customized industrial training
  Expedited provision of site-specific infrastructure
  Help with regulatory problems

New Wave Economic Development Policies
(Primarily Targeted at Small or Existing Businesses)

Capital Market Programs
  Predominantly government-financed loan or equity programs
  Government support for predominantly privately financed loan or equity
    programs
Information/Education for Small Business
  Small-business ombudsman/information office
  Community college classes in starting a business
  Small-business development centers
  Entrepreneurial training programs
  Small-business incubators
Research and High Technology
  Centers of excellence in business-related research at public universities
  Research-oriented industrial parks
  Applied research grants
  Technology transfer programs/industrial extension services
Export Assistance
  Information/training in how to export
  Trade missions
  Export financing

Source: Bartik (1991:4).

New-wave policies also are directed at reducing business costs, but they go far beyond that to involve an "interventionist" state seeking to create new markets, products, and industry (Gray and Lowery 1990). Bartik describes these policies as follows:

> What I call "new wave" economic development policies are an eclectic group of policies that became popular in many states during the late 1970s and early 1980s. These policies encourage various forms of innovation, such as applied research, industrial modernization, entrepreneurship, and business expansion into export markets. They also have in common a willingness to involve government much more with business decisions. Rather than just providing cash, they would have government provide services to businesses to help them determine their best market or technology. (1991:5)

A similar classification of economic development policies is provided by Eisenger (1988) and is presented in Table 2.2. Supply-side policies are

Table 2.2. Contrasts between Traditional Supply-Side Policy and Demand-Side Entrepreneurial Policy

Supply Side	Demand Side
Growth is promoted by lowering production-factor costs through government subsidies of capital and land and through low taxes.	Growth is promoted by discovering, expanding, developing, or creating new markets for local goods and services.
Main focus is on established, potentially mobile capital.	Main focus is on new capital
Strategies focus on stimulating capital relocation or capital retention.	Strategies focus on new business formation and small business expansion.
Development involves competition with other jurisdictions for the same investment.	Development proceeds by nurturing indigenous resources.
Government supports low-risk undertakings.	Government becomes involved in high-risk enterprises and activities.
Any employer is a suitable target for development assistance.	Development assistance is offered selectively according to strategic criteria.
Government's role is to follow and support private-sector decisions about where to invest, what businesses will be profitable, and what products will sell.	Government's role is to help identify investment opportunities that the private sector may either have overlooked or be reluctant to pursue, including opportunities in new markets, new products, and new industries.

Source: Eisenger (1988:12).

the traditional approaches and demand-side policies reflect the more recent new-wave approaches followed by many states. Both Bartik and Eisenger recognize that traditional/supply-side policies are more likely to redistribute jobs rather than create new ones. Firms that leave one area to move to a more favorable location simply change the location of unemployment. In contrast, new-wave/demand-side policies have the potential to create more jobs in the long run because they encourage innovation and growth. But regardless of the particular strategies followed, all development policies are assessed in terms of their ability to create jobs.

Some analysts have used the contrast between traditional and new-wave policies to argue for a commitment to a broad range of actions by government, education, labor, and capital to move toward a high-technology economy composed of smaller firms, a highly skilled labor force, and targeted government subsidies. Osborne (1988), for example, has pointed to a number of state-level actions that have acknowledged the demands of global competition and technological change and have been designed to transform state economic activity. Among the innovations discussed are

1. public venture capital funds to stimulate projects that are too costly for individual entrepreneurs or too risky for private capital;
2. programs to stimulate technical innovations such as academic-business projects for technology transfer, and government-sponsored research in areas of global competition;
3. educational programs that go beyond literacy and numeracy to emphasize lifelong learning and continual acquisition of new skills; and
4. business-labor-management agreements to restructure labor-management relations to increase worker participation, productivity, and job security.

The response of state and local governments to the fiscal crisis created by deindustrialization has been to search for ways to stimulate economic development, create jobs, and increase tax revenue. Many states are trying some new ways of attracting business and stimulating growth. The question of who benefits from these activities must remain unanswered until we have had time to assess the results of the policies that have been tried in states across the country. Until we have the answer to this bottom-line question we will focus on a prior question: How does a new approach to economic growth develop in a state and how does that idea take hold among the various interest groups with a stake in growth-related projects? In this book we examine six major development projects undertaken to attract Japanese auto assembly plants. These projects appear to represent a mixture of traditional and new-wave incentives and they are presented to the public with great hope for growth. We hope that by examining these six projects we will get a glimpse of the emerging political economy.

THEORIZING CHANGE: THE EMERGING
POLITICAL ECONOMY

The United States has lost its place as a world leader in manufacturing, and as a result has eliminated millions of high-wage, secure jobs that have supported the belief in the American Dream of expanding opportunities in a predominantly middle class society. Multinational corporations circle the globe in search of the best opportunities for profit. Sometimes the search results in locating production facilities outside the United States, and sometimes it results in mergers and acquisitions that produce paper profits but not new jobs and growth. Our greatest competitors, the Japanese, believe that we have turned away from making quality products for domestic consumption and export, and have become obsessed with short-term profits. Akio Morita, chairman of Sony Corporation, feels that engineers concerned with technical innovation have been replaced by MBAs, lawyers, and professional moneymakers who trade in the value of the Japanese yen, German mark, or British pound (*New York Times*, June 6, 1987). As a result of this internationalization of capital markets and production, the United States has become a debtor nation dependent on imports to satisfy consumer demand.

The position taken in this book is that the changes precipitated by deindustrialization and the emerging global economy are not simply routine or minor changes of an otherwise robust economy. Rather, we believe that we are experiencing a significant and historic transformation in the way that political and economic life is organized. The transplant phenomenon illustrates one aspect of this transformation, in that it represents the emergence of a new regional economy based on close cooperation between private corporations and state governments.

A number of analysts have viewed the changes of the last two decades as transformative in nature, and they have provided different outlines of a way of thinking about the transition. Gordon, Edwards, and Reich (1982) present the most general framework for understanding three major structural changes in the organization of work and the development of capitalism in the United States. The authors contend that capitalism's development has moved through three overlapping stages of about fifty years each. The stage of *initial proletarianization*, from the 1820s to the 1890s, was characterized by the creation of wage earning workers who had to sell their potential to work to an employer. The potential to work was transformed into actual work through a simple system of control expressed through close supervision. The *homogenization* period, from 1870 to World War II, brought a transformation of work and labor markets caused by standardization of the labor process and more systematic forms of technical and bureaucratic control of workers. Assembly line production and extreme specialization reduced worker's control over the labor process and led to an increase in labor unrest. The *segmentation* period, from the 1920s to the present, is characterized by the creation of three distinct labor markets that differ in terms of skill level of workers, the system of control used to get work done, and the extent of wage and job security.

These three stages are discussed by the authors as follows:

> We propose more specifically that overlapping stages of *initial proletarianization, homogenization,* and *segmentation* have shaped the development of the labor process and labor markets in the United States since the early nineteenth century. Each of these stages crystallized when an economic crisis, not unlike the present crisis, was resolved through the emergence of a new institutional structure that restarted a period of rapid economic growth. The process through which these institutional structures emerged again, not unlike the process of restructuring that we now see beginning in the current period—involved continuing and intense class conflict. (Gordon et al. 1982:3)

For present purposes, the most important aspect of the Gordon et al. framework is that each stage in the development of capitalism is characterized by a distinct *social structure of accumulation* (SSA) that provides the institutional arrangements for the accumulation of capital. Each SSA includes the laws and values that define the rights of capital and of labor; it includes the tax codes, and fiscal and monetary policies that encourage capital investment; it includes the competitive and cooperative relations among firms involved in providing each other with goods and services; and it provides a setting of interorganizational relations in the public and private sectors that foster the search for innovations in the production of goods and services. In short, the "social structure of accumulation consists of all the institutions that impinge upon the accumulation process" (Gordon et al. 1982:23).

Within each stage in the process of capitalist development Gordon et al. hypothesize that the institutional arrangements that comprise the social structure of accumulation go through a cycle of "exploration, consolidation, and decay." As the institutional arrangements in a particular historical period confront a period of stagnation, capitalists will search for new arrangements that will solve the problems that limit capital accumulation.

This is exploration. When the new institutional arrangements are seen as solutions to crisis, there will be a period of consolidation, or rapid capital accumulation and expanding profits. These new arrangements will eventually exhaust their capacity to expand capital accumulation and will become impediments to accumulation thereby leading to decay.

Although this framework put forward by Gordon et al. is very general and covers long historical periods, it does urge us to see the long list of changes related to deindustrialization as part of a pattern of the decay of one social structure of accumulation and the emergence of new institutional arrangements for capital accumulation. Thus, the mobility of capital and the attacks on organized labor are designed to establish new labor-management agreements because prior accords were limiting profits to unacceptable levels. Similarly, capital's threat to invest outside the United States encouraged federal and state governments to reduce the costs of doing business through tax adjustments and relaxed regulatory standards. The emerging pattern of cooperation between multinational corporations and state governments represented by the transplant phenomenon is an example of a new institutional arrangement for capital accumulation. In order for this new pattern to work, the state must have legal legitimacy for its entrepreneurial role, it must have political support from competing interest groups in the state, and it must have public support for the corporatist project. Throughout the remainder of this book we will see how the emerging social structure of accumulation begins to take shape in the six states in the Midwest corridor.

With the consolidation of these changes there should be improvements in economic growth followed by new forces of resistance that seek to restrict the gains of capital. While this is not exactly a predictive framework, it does contribute to a coherent understanding of historical change.

Another framework for understanding the transformation of our economy is provided by Piore and Sabel (1984), who argue that we are currently experiencing the "second industrial divide" (the first industrial divide coming in the nineteenth century with the mass production technologies). Piore and Sabel believe that "the present deterioration in economic performance results from the limits of the model of industrial development that is founded on mass production: the use of special purpose (product-specific) machines and of semiskilled workers to produce standardized goods" (p. 4).

The exhaustion of mass production technology as the key to growth takes us to a situation where there are two paths to future growth. The first path calls for rebuilding the strengths of mass production through efforts by multinational corporations to stabilize markets and create new forms of global cooperation. The second path is what Piore and Sable call flexible specialization:

a strategy of permanent innovation: accommodation to ceaseless change, rather than an effort to control it.. . .[a strategy] based on flexible—multi-use—equipment; skilled workers; and the creation through politics, of an industrial community that restricts the forms of competition to those favoring innovation (p. 17)

Some of the characteristics of flexible specialization are similar to the lean production that is practiced in the Japanese auto industry.

Although these paths to growth may be contradictory, Piore and Sabel explore the possibility that mass production and flexible specialization may be "combined in a unified *international* economy" (p. 279). Small firms using advanced technologies might flourish in the current industrialized nations, and traditional mass production systems might be based in less developed nations. Moreover, the authors also explore several different ways of flexible specialization in the United States, such as industrial districts composed of many small firms in the same industry, e.g., Silicon Valley or the garment industry.

The point to be emphasized here is that the second industrial divide does not necessarily require a choice between contradictory strategies for growth, but the coexistence of strategies that are suited to particular locations and opportunities. A focus on the variety of ways in which capital accumulation is undertaken is emphasized in the work of Harvey (1989), who examines the new systems of production and the mode of social and political regulation (which he calls a "regime of accumulation") that are replacing the mass production of Fordism.

Harvey posits a shift from the rigidities of mass production–mass consumption to a system of *flexible accumulation*, which

rests on flexibility with respect to labour processes, labour markets, products, and patterns of consumption.. . .It has entrained rapid shifts in the patterning of uneven development, both between sectors and between geographical regions, giving rise, for example, to a vast surge in so-called "service sector" employment as well as entirely new industrial ensembles in hitherto underdeveloped regions. (p. 147)

The idea of flexible accumulation is consistent with what is known about the changing capital markets and technological change. The rapid restructuring of the U.S. economy has been facilitated by new technologies in production that provide flexibility in adapting to a variety of production tasks (e.g., computer-assisted design and manufacturing), and advances in telecommunications and computer information systems that facilitate coordination across spatially separated activities in production and distribution (Shaiken 1984; Castells and Henderson 1987).

The emerging political economy of the United States appears to be a mosaic of forms that are not manifestly affine according to theoretical formulations. The combination of mobile capital and technological innovation produces a variety of specific forms of spatial and industrial restructuring by the way that it interacts with the attributes of territorial areas (e.g., availability of labor, transportation, markets, suppliers). Cities, states, and regions are hit by plant closings, plant openings, new sweatshops, white-collar employment and corporate command cities (i.e., headquarters of multinational firms), and the appearance of research and development laboratories (Smith 1987). The mixture of mass production, shop production, craft workers, and traditional paternalistic labor relations (to name just a few of the different forms of production and control) are the product of global capital markets and technological change.

In this book we examine how the changing global economy has impacted the political and economic life of a six-state region of the United States. The new flexibility of capital accumulation at first produced industrial decline in the region by moving manufacturing to lower wage areas, and then made it the center of a new production complex of Japanese auto assembly plants and suppliers. The Midwest corridor has been both the victim and the beneficiary of the changing global economy. In the span of about a dozen years this region has faced major deindustrialization, followed by the intervention of international capital and a new production system. The establishment of auto transplants in the six-state region provides the opportunity to observe how international capital, local state initiatives for economic development, and community politics interact to create a unique form of social and economic action.

We believe that our case study approach will provide a glimpse of how the broad theoretical formulations of global change are reflected in the day-to-day actions of politicians, business owners, labor officials, environmentalists, and other community members trying to benefit from, or protect themselves against, the seeming vagaries of the changing political economy.

Chapter 3

Settling in the Heartland:
Why the Midwest Corridor?

(with Fanying Kong)

In short, we believe Lafayette and Tippecanoe County is a wholesome place to live, work and raise a family.

Lafayette was picked because of its transportation facilities and because it is near major automotive supply manufacturers.

We wanted to be sure that we could obtain enough skilled labor force. That was the deciding factor.

All of the above statements were made on December 3, 1986, by Akira Soejima, senior managing director for Fuji Motors. The occasion was a press conference in Lafayette, Indiana, at which he was participating in the announcement that the Subaru-Isuzu (SIA) plant would be built in Indiana. Other Japanese executives in the 1980s made similar statements about why Toyota selected Kentucky or Nissan selected Tennessee as the site for a transplant. All of the above statements may be the real reasons for selecting a particular state, or none of them may be.

In this chapter we try to answer the complex question of why the transplants chose to locate in the six states in the Midwest corridor. This is no easy task, since the decision-makers in each transplant have not made public announcements as to why they chose Tennessee or Indiana as the site for their plant in the United States. Lacking this direct knowledge, we will address the question of location choice by comparing each of the states that attracted a transplant (winner states) with the states that were in the final stage of the selection process (competitor states). We analyze six cases of winner-competitor comparisons in order to see if and how the winners and competitors are different. If we observe a pattern of differences between winner and competitor states we may be able to answer

41

the "why" question. This is how we shall proceed. But first we must decide on the characteristics of states that will be used in our comparison of winners and competitors.

The conventional approach to understanding the location decision of a firm is to view the firm as a rational actor trying to match the economic and noneconomic features of a possible site against some preestablished set of needs that are ordered as to priority. Thus, firms seeking an industrial site will consider labor factors (quality and cost), proximity to markets, transportation, quality of life indicators (educational system, climate, recreational facilities), and business climate (taxes, regulations). The importance of these factors will differ across firms and at different stages in the process of making a location choice (Blair and Premus 1987). Market and transportation factors may be important in choosing between regions, but quality of life may be more important when choosing a state or a site within a state.

This approach to studying industrial location decisions provides an important foundation for research on the topic, but it needs modification when applied to the case of transplants. Several aspects of the transplant phenomenon call for this modification:

1. Conventional location theory views the firm as the active party making the location decision, and cities or states as a passive bundle of characteristics. Clearly, the firm makes the location decision, but cities and states today are required to be active and even aggressive in their pursuit of new industry. The ability of a state to deliver on both contractual agreements (e.g., tax abatements) and promises for the future is a matter of communicating that ability in the context of relations of trust. Thus, the way that a governor is perceived as a person by Japanese executives may outweigh many traditional location factors.

2. As noted in Chapter 1, Japanese auto firms decided to build assembly plants in the United States because of growing political pressure that threatened to limit the importation of Japanese cars. Japanese corporations became painfully aware of the need to influence state and national political systems to respond to the needs of foreign auto plants. Thus, the location choices of the transplants may have given high priority to the Japanese corporations developing their influence among U.S. politicians, an outcome that is more likely in six contiguous states than in six widely dispersed locations.

This is not to say that Honda, Nissan, Mazda, Mitsubishi, Toyota, and Fuji-Isuzu collectively decided to locate in six contiguous states. But the location decision of each company was made separately, and the reasons for the choices of Honda and Nissan in early 1980s may be different from those of Toyota and Fuji-Isuzu in late 1980s. The latter two decisions completed the puzzle, so to speak, creating a production complex of extraordinary economic and political power in the Midwest corridor.

3. The decision by Japanese auto companies to come to the United States took place in the context of general anti-Japanese sentiment about the growing economic strength of Japan in relation to the United States. Trade deficits, increasing auto imports, unemployment in the auto industry, and penetration of markets once dominated by the United States shaped the climate of opinion regarding United States-Japan relationships. The transplant companies would be understandably sensitive to the kind of reception they might receive from people in host communities. The nature of community sentiment toward the Japanese is likely to influence political officials to be more or less cooperative, to encourage workers to be more or less committed employees, and to shape the experiences of Japanese management and their families.

These special aspects of the transplant phenomenon require that we expand the conventional framework for understanding location decisions to include a broader range of economic, political, and social forces that impinge upon the transplants. Support for our view that the location decisions of Japanese transplants represent a special case is found in Milward and Newman's (1989) review of research literature on location decisions. Research on the location decisions of U.S. firms points to the importance of traditional factors such as labor productivity, transportation, land availability and cost, corporate tax rates, and unionization. In contrast, a study by Yoshida (1987) of Japanese company executives involved in selecting a U.S. plant site reports that the most significant location factors were labor productivity, proximity to markets, level of union activity, and the history of management-labor relationships in a region. Moreover, it is reported that "during site investigations, the Japanese firms were interested in the local community's attitude toward their direct investments" (p. 207). Glickman and Woodward report that "Japanese investors in particular place great importance on 'being wanted by a locality" (1989:232) when making a site selection. Such considerations go beyond traditional location theory.

THREE PERSPECTIVES ON LOCATION DECISIONS: ORGANIZATION, CLASS, AND STATE INFLUENCES

An organization perspective of location decisions proceeds from the established proposition that organizations cannot generate internally all the resources required for maintaining the system. Therefore it is necessary for organizations to obtain needed resources or services by entering into transactions or relationships with elements of their environment (Aldrich and Pfeffer 1976). Because of competition among organizations, and uncertainty as to future supply of needed resources, the search for stable resources is a key element in making strategic decisions. The larger the organization and the greater the commitment of capital to a project, the greater the need to have a predictable supply of resources.

Since all firms need to acquire resources from their environment and to stabilize such exchanges, they are subject to external control and constraint. Access to external resources is an especially critical problem for foreign firms since their successful operations mainly depend on a host environment that is relatively unfamiliar. Foreign firms have special difficulties in acquiring resources because they are both new and culturally different. They face a situation of uncertain market, a shortage of resources, and an overarching policy concern for interorganizational coordination and reduction of instability. The latter concern is generated by relations with suppliers, labor, governmental authorities, and community figures involved in the interrelationships.

Lack of resources restricts the amount of power that foreign firms can exercise over market and competitive conditions (Romanelli 1989). Thus, foreign firms have little ability to improve the environment they face because of the time needed to achieve such effectiveness. From an environmental perspective, the likelihood that new firms can overcome these difficulties depends on the extent of available resources in an environment. Such availability will affect the amount and kind of resources that a foreign manufacturing firm can acquire. Therefore, a manufacturing firm's location and its ability to keep competition to a minimum as well as to maintain a steady flow of supplies to serve its needs are critical to its success.

Foreign firms want to create the environments to which they adapt by selecting the site they will locate—by excluding some elements of the environment and including others. The task environment includes the supply of raw materials, which is critical to the firm's production inputs. Transportation is a cost of production that is a function not only of distance but also of time. The limitations of a site's physical environment— road and rail links—that affect transporting production input and output must be considered. Along with economic conditions, investors need constantly to consider a site's social environment—the surrounding population, including availability of labor with suitable education and skills. The relative availability, cost, and productivity of labor can dominate the location decision for foreign transplant firms since the ratio of labor costs to total production costs is relatively high for automobile assembly production. Productivity and work ethic of the labor force are of critical importance to foreign companies that promote their products on the basis of quality.

The quality of life in the community assumes great importance, particularly when the plant involves large numbers of management-level personnel. To foreign companies quality of life considerations may be even more important. Jane Little (1980) cites the example of a Japanese company, locating in Connecticut, that expressed serious concern about where the children of thirty Japanese managers would go to school.

There are several hypotheses on the ways Japanese automakers may act that are consistent with an organization/resource dependency perspective. Foreign transplant decision-makers must be concerned with the issue of resource procurement. They will be extremely attentive to those resources that are crucial to a firm's profit making (as well as to sustaining and/or expanding a firm's productivity). The organizational model suggests that foreign transplants will select sites that deliver the greatest amount of needed resources, the best educated/trained/motivated work force, and the most favorable quality of life amenities for managers and their families. While wage levels and unionization are important considerations, they represent uncertain quantities in the foreseeable future. The prudent corporate decision-maker will be influenced by what is more certain and more controllable factors.

We will compare winner and competitor states on the importance of the organization perspective by examining the following characteristics of states:

1. Number of auto supplier firms (SIC 3711, 3714, 3011, 3465, 3592, 3647, 3694. Source: Census of Manufacturers)
2. Interstate highway miles (Source: U.S. Federal Highway Administration)
3. Electricity rates for industrial users (dollars per million BTUs. Source: State Energy Price and Expenditure Report)
4. Gas rates for industrial users (dollars per million BTUs. Source: Statistical Abstract of the United States)
5. Number of colleges and universities (Source: National Center for Education Statistics Education Directory)
6. Number of industrial technology graduates (Source: National Association of Industrial Technology Programs)
7. Per pupil expenditures, primary and secondary education (Source: National Center for Education Statistics)
8. State parks/recreation acreage per capita (Source: Statistical Abstracts of the United States)
9. Doctors per hundred thousand population (Source: County and City Data Book)

10. Median housing cost (Source: County and City Data Book)
11. Crime rate per hundred thousand population (Source: Uniform Crime Reports for the United States)

In the class perspective the investment decisions of firms must be understood in terms of the inherent conflict between management and labor in a capitalist system of production. The opportunities for capital accumulation are greater when firms can exercise control over wages and the labor process. The relative organizational power and militancy of labor is one of the most important factors limiting the actions of management, and therefore influences corporate investment decisions. The existence of strong unions also provides workers with political power for achieving economic well-being independent of the organization for which they work (Coleman 1988).

The level of strike activity in a state provides quantitative evidence about the state of labor-capital relations and working-class militancy. Chronic absenteeism, work slowdowns, and turnover rates are also evidence of working-class grievances and discontent, but only strike data have been recorded with sufficient regularity to be used in this study.

Another feature of the class perspective that is linked to the strength of organized labor is the extent to which states contribute to the social wage in the form of unemployment benefits, public assistance, and disability insurance. Since the state-funded portion of these programs must be financed from taxes, the more generous welfare states tend to have higher corporate and personal tax rates. The joint effect of higher taxes and welfare expenditures is to slow down economic growth. It is expected that transplants will seek to locate in states with lower wage, antiunion, and weak social wage environments. We will compare winner and competitor states on the importance of the class perspective by examining the following characteristics.

1. Percent of nonagricultural labor force that is unionized (Source: Union Sourcebook, Industrial Relations Data and Information Services)
2. Number of work stoppages (Source: Handbook of Labor Statistics)
3. Unemployment rate
4. Average hourly wages of production workers in manufacturing (Source: Handbook of Labor Statistics)
5. Per capita personal income
6. Workman's compensation benefits: Maximum payment per week for temporary total disability
7. Welfare expenditures per capita (Source: U.S. Bureau of the Census)
8. Unemployment benefits: Percentage of weekly wage (Source: U.S. Employment and Training Administration)

The state perspective starts with the proposition that the primary function of the state is to maintain political and economic order (Block 1987). Since the state depends on a reasonable level of economic activity and a favorable environment for capital accumulation, it seeks close cooperation with business to further economic growth. Economic well-being and political strength go hand in hand, and the political regime in power will tend to pursue policies that are in the general interests of capital. Public support for a regime is closely tied with the level of economic activity, especially the employment rate. A serious drop in the level of economic activity, along with a parallel rise in unemployment, reduces the public support for the regime, and increases the likelihood that the state regime will be removed from power, or it will increase the challenges to the regime and decrease its political ability to take effective actions. The capacity of the state to finance itself through taxation or borrowing also depends on the state of the economy: If economic activity is in decline, the state will have difficulty maintaining its revenues at an adequate level (Lindblom 1977).

Private corporations thus have major impact on the state's economic activities. When a big corporation decides to locate a branch plant in a given locale, it sets the conditions for the surrounding land use pattern and extends employment opportunities (Molotch 1976). Therefore, state managers have a direct interest in using their power to facilitate investment. There is a tendency for state agencies to orient their various programs toward the goal of facilitating and encouraging private investment (Block 1987).

Besides the efforts to create physical conditions that can best serve industrial growth, states also attempt to maintain the kind of business climate that attracts industry. More and more states introduce state legislation that has a profound effect on the business climate. Through tax laws and legislation of industrial financing and worker's compensation, state policymakers are playing an increasing role of determining a state's posture toward business. The state managers realize that favorable taxation, vocational training, law enforcement, and "good" labor relations are attractive to investors. They not only affect business profitability, but also serve as indicators of a state's attitude toward business. Government also is a key contributor to the political climate since its everyday activities are watched by the potential foreign investor. While there is much debate about the effect of financial incentives on the location decision, few would dispute the value of such incentives as expressions of government attitudes. This is important to Japanese auto transplant decision-makers, who in their home country are accustomed to dealing with government.

While business concerns have always been at the forefront of a site selection process, state government decisions are also involved. Plant-location decisions are made with reference to such issues as labor costs, tax rates, and the costs of transporting goods to markets, and it is government decisions that help determine such costs. Government decisions influence the cost of overhead expenses (e.g., pollution abatement requirements, employee safety standards) and affect the costs of labor through indirect manipulation of unemployment rates, through the use of police to constrain or enhance union organizing, and through the legislation and administration of welfare laws (Piven and Cloward 1972). Businesses are generally mindful of these governmental powers.

State agencies usually reflect what state governments do (Dye 1985). The growth of state bureaucracies represents the expanding scope of the role of state government. Several government agencies provide information that is of interest and importance to state and local governments in attracting foreign firms. The main organization charged with this responsibility is typically an office of foreign investment within a state's department of commerce or community development, a state's department of economic development, or the office of a governor or mayor. These agencies maintain accurate data that are readily available upon request, thus reducing the cost and time involved in searching for answers to questions that might arise during negotiations with a specific investor. The responsiveness of an agency to a foreign investor's initial questions often determines whether negotiations continue. Since states and localities have many incentive options, those agencies often have the initial contact with prospective foreign investors. In addition, they generally refer investors to particularly attractive locations and "package" incentives to meet specific needs.

The role of the state in economic development leads us to ask two questions about a state's administrative capacities and political regime: (1) Is there an administrative apparatus that can facilitate economic development and industrial recruitment? (2) Is there a stable political regime to follow through on agreements? Since political regimes will pursue economic growth as a means of solidifying and extending political control, states with a strong administrative apparatus and dominant political control will be better able to develop and deliver a credible economic incentive package to attract foreign investments.

We compare winner and competitor states on the importance of the state perspective by examining the following characteristics of states:

1. Party affiliation of governor, last five terms (Source: Book of the States)
2. Party composition of state house of representatives, last five terms
3. Party composition of state senate, last five terms
4. Number of state government units (Source: State Policy Data Book)

5. State appropriations for international business development (Source: National Association of State Development Agencies)
6. Number of staff working on foreign investment recruitment
7. Number of overseas economic development offices
8. Number of tax incentives available for industry (Source: Industrial Development and Site Selection Handbook)
9. Number of financial assistance programs available for industry
10. Total taxes per capita (Source: U.S. Bureau of the Census, Governmental Finances)
11. Property taxes per capita (Source: Census of Government, Governmental Finances)

The three perspectives on location decisions outlined above—organizational, class, and state—provide three general answers to the question of why auto transplants selected the six states in the Midwest corridor as the sites for their new U.S. production plants. We do not expect the three answers to be mutually exclusive, but we do expect that a combination of factors from the three perspectives will help us to understand the location choices.

It is important to reemphasize that location decisions can take place in stages, and that different characteristics of regions or states will be of importance at different times in the decision process. Since we are studying the final stage in the process—when Japanese firms were deciding among a small number of finalists—it is possible that some of the factors from the three perspectives were important at an earlier decision stage (e.g., choosing a region in which to locate) but not in choosing among finalists. With that caveat in mind we proceed to examine winner and competitor states.

WINNERS AND COMPETITORS

Table 3.1 contains a listing of the six states that attracted transplants and the states that were in the final competition for the new plants. Each winner-competitor cluster will permit us to compare states on the characteristics described above that reflect the organization, class, and state perspectives of location decisions. Table 3.1 also presents the unemployment rates for each state, along with the national unemployment rate. An examination of unemployment rates will permit us to see if the severity of economic recession of the 1980s was a factor in inducing states to compete for transplants. It will also allow us to see if the winners were experiencing greater unemployment than competitors, and therefore worked harder to attract transplants.

Table 3.1. Unemployment Rates (%) for Winner and Competitor States[a]
(Rates for Year of Site Selection and Four Preceding Years)

Winner/competitors	Year 4	Year 3	Year 2	Year 1	Site selection
Ohio (1980)	7.8	6.5	5.4	5.9	8.4
Arizona	9.8	8.2	6.1	5.1	6.7
Indiana	6.1	5.7	5.7	6.4	9.6
Kentucky	5.6	4.7	5.2	5.6	8.0
Missouri	6.2	5.9	5.0	4.5	7.2
(National rate)	(7.9)	(7.1)	(5.9)	(5.8)	(7.4)
Tennessee (1980)	6.0	6.3	5.8	5.8	7.3
Georgia	8.1	6.9	5.7	5.1	6.4
South Carolina	6.9	7.2	5.7	5.0	6.9
(National rate)	(7.9)	(7.1)	(5.9)	(5.8)	(7.4)
Michigan (1984)	12.4	12.3	15.5	14.2	11.2
Alabama	8.8	10.7	14.4	13.7	11.1
Iowa	5.8	6.9	8.5	8.5	7.0
Kansas	4.5	4.2	6.3	6.1	5.2
Missouri	7.2	7.7	9.2	9.9	7.2
Nebraska	4.1	4.1	6.1	5.7	4.4
North Carolina	6.6	6.4	9.0	8.9	6.7
Oklahoma	4.8	3.6	5.7	9.0	7.0
South Carolina	6.9	8.4	10.0	10.0	7.1
Tennessee	7.3	9.1	11.8	11.5	8.6
(National rate)	(7.4)	(7.7)	(10.1)	(9.9)	(7.4)
Illinois (1985)	8.5	11.3	11.4	9.1	9.0
Indiana	10.1	11.9	11.1	8.6	7.9
Michigan	12.3	15.5	14.2	11.2	9.9
Ohio	9.6	12.5	12.2	9.4	8.9
(National rate)	(7.7)	(10.1)	(9.9)	(7.4)	(7.2)
Kentucky (1985)	8.4	10.6	11.7	9.3	9.5
Georgia	6.4	7.8	7.5	6.0	6.5
Indiana	10.1	11.9	11.1	8.6	7.9
Kansas	4.2	6.3	6.1	5.2	5.0
Missouri	7.7	9.2	9.9	7.2	6.4
Tennessee	9.1	11.8	11.5	8.6	8.0
(National rate)	(7.7)	(10.1)	(9.9)	(7.4)	(7.2)
Indiana (1986)	11.9	11.1	8.6	7.9	6.7
Illinois	11.3	11.4	9.1	9.0	8.1
Kentucky	10.6	11.7	9.3	9.5	9.3
(National rate)	(10.1)	(9.9)	(7.4)	(7.2)	(7.0)

Sources: U.S. Department of Commerce (1989); Bureau of Labor Statistics, *Unemployment in States and Local Areas, 1977–1986* (microfiche)
[a]Winners listed first in each group.

Several patterns can be seen in Table 3.1. In four of the six cases (Michigan, Illinois, Kentucky, and Indiana) winner states and many competitor states had unemployment rates that exceeded national rates in the years preceding the location choice decision. This pattern is not found in the Ohio and Tennessee cases, and it is interesting that these were the two earliest sites selected for transplants. The economic and political climate for both Japanese auto firms and U.S. states was perhaps less critical at that time than during the mid-1980s.

A second pattern in the unemployment rates is that the winner states did not have more severe unemployment than their competitors. Only Michigan is an exception to this pattern, revealing much greater unemployment than the competitor states and the national rate.

In the next section, each winner state is examined in comparison to the finalist states that were their competitors for transplants. The focus is on the critical differences between the winner and competitors within each case. The consistent patterns across the comparisons for each case are identified and discussed. The critical differences between the winner and competitors will be highlighted in each table. The other variables that do not exhibit a consistent pattern will be excluded from discussion.

OHIO CASE

Ohio was one of the five finalists that were the candidates for the site of Honda North American. The other four competing states are Arizona, Indiana, Kentucky and Missouri. Although the intensive competition for the Honda automobile investment happened around 1980, the new investment of $250 million was actually an expansion of a $35 million motorcycle manufacturing plant that was announced in 1977 and began production in 1979. At the time the motorcycle manufacturing plant site was chosen, a nearby auto plant was under consideration if the motorcycle manufacturing plant was successful. Based on such background, we do not know how much the other states could do to relocate Honda from Marysville, Ohio, where the Honda motorcycle manufacturing plant is located.

Considering the data gathered for this study, the most impressive factor under the organization perspective is that Ohio has more auto supplier firms than the other states (see Table 3.2). The location of Honda auto assembly transplants within Ohio took advantage of the concentration of supplier firms in the state, which ensures just-in-time deliveries of components and materials—the manufacturing system operated in Japan. Table 3.2 also shows that Ohio has a lot more higher education institu-

Table 3.2. Ohio Case—Organization Perspective[a]

	OH	AZ	IN	KY	MO
Auto suppliers (1977)	226	4	117	27	45
Highway miles (thousands; 1980)	111.1	75.2	91.5	69.3	118.5
Electricity rate (1982)	5.61	6.85	4.66	6.38	6.41
Gas rate (1980)	2.97	2.40	2.59	2.67	2.51
Colleges and universities (1980)	135	28	74	52	86
Industrial technology grads (1984/1985)	204	35	471	198	790
Dollars per pupil (1980)	2,973	2,824	2,697	2,437	2,774
Park acreage per capita, ranked (1984)	43	42	45	40	33
Doctors per 100,000 (1980)	153.0	170.7	122.6	125.8	152.2
Median home price (1980)	45,100	56,600	37,200	34,200	36,700
Crime per 100,000 (1980)	5,431	8,171	4,930	3,434	5,433

[a]Number in parentheses is the year of the data.

tions than the other states. Its education expenditure per pupil is also greater than competitor states. Ohio's gas price is higher than other competing states, but fuels and electricity prices for industrial users are at the low end compared with all but one of the other states.

Turning to the state perspective, Table 3.3 shows that Ohio has more government units than the other states, and also invests more money to attract international business. Its international budget for state economic development, number of staff devoted to international business, and number of overseas offices all outnumbered other competitor states. These may be some of the reasons that brought the first Japanese auto investment into Ohio. The economic incentives offered by Ohio may also have played an important role in attracting Japanese investment. Our data show that Ohio outperformed all the other competitors regarding the number of tax incentives and financial assistance offered to industry during 1979 and 1980.

Table 3.4 contains variables associated with the class perspective. Ohio is at the high end for several variables including percentage of labor force in unions, number of work stoppages, hourly wage rate, per capita income level, workers' compensation and unemployment benefits. These are the factors that capital should try to avoid when considering invest-

Table 3.3. Ohio Case—State Perspective[a]

	OH	AZ	IN	KY	MO
Governor's party	DDRDR	RRDDD	RRRRR	DDDDD	DRRDD
House party	ddddd	rrrrr	rrdrr	dDDDD	ddddd
Senate party	rrddd	rrddr	rrrdr	dDDDD	ddddd
Number of government units (1982)	3,394	453	2,866	1,242	3,118
International budget ($1000s; 1984)	1,900	200	560	838	580
Number of staff foreign recruitment (1984)	39	5	12	5.5	10.5
Number of overseas offices (1986)	3	0	3	1	2
Tax incentives (1980)	10	6	8	7	6
Financial assistance programs (1980)	10	1	8	8	6
Property tax per capita ($, 1980)	281	352	246	135	215
Total tax per capita ($, 1982)	973	1,060	876	855	843

[a]The time periods for political party affiliation of state governor and state legislatures are five terms preceding the transplant announcing year. These are same for all the cases.

Code for house and senate: D, 75% or more Democratic (strong majority); d, 51–74% Democratic (simple majority); r, 51–74% Republican; R, 75% or more Republican.

Table 3.4. Ohio Case—Class Perspective[a]

	OH	AZ	IN	KY	MO
Union (%)	30.0	14.9	29.5	12.8	28.8
Number of work stoppages	384	22	137	109	88
Unemployment	8.4	6.7	9.6	8.0	7.2
Hourly wage	8.57	7.29	8.49	7.34	7.26
Per capita income	9,462	7,268	8,936	7,613	8,982
Weekly workman's compensation benefit	258.0	192.3	130.0	131.0	125.0
Welfare ($ per capita)	169	68	121	177	134
Unemployment benefits (% of weekly wage)	44.6	32.3	31.0	40.3	33.9

[a]All the data in this table are for 1980.

ment. On the other hand, these factors are usually associated with the industrial heartland which contains the skilled labor force and established industrial infrastructure needed by an auto plant. In addition, Honda's experience with labor at their motorcycle plant in Ohio may have led them to discount potential for unionization and conflict.

There are a number of qualitative factors that should be considered when trying to understand why Ohio was selected to be the site for the Honda auto plant. Gelsanliter (1992:17-18) reports that in 1976 Governor James Rhodes and Director of Development James Duerk learned that an unnamed Japanese auto company was conducting a study to examine possibilities for building an auto plant in the United States. Rhodes and Duerk made a hasty trip to Japan to meet with executives of Toyota, Nissan, and Honda and to tell them why Ohio was the right place. This type of active, committed governor may have been an important factor when Honda got around to selecting a site.

In summary, the Ohio case points to the importance of several factors that may have favored Ohio over competitors. First, related to the goal of building automobiles, Ohio excelled in its auto supplier infrastructure. Second, the state's administrative capacity for pursuing foreign investment and providing a variety of financial incentives was greater than that available from competitor states. This capacity combined with an activist governor may tell the Ohio story.

TENNESSEE CASE

The competition for the Nissan plant was intense, involving Tennessee, Georgia, and South Carolina as the final list. Regarding the automobile industrial infrastructure, Tennessee is closer to the existing auto agglomeration in the Midwest. It also has more auto parts and accessory firms than Georgia and South Carolina (see Table 3.5). Although its electricity price for industry is relatively high, Tennessee's gas price for industry is the lowest among the three states. It has slightly more higher education institutions and a larger number of industrial technology graduates compared to Georgia and South Carolina. Tennessee also has the highest number of physicians per hundred thousand population and the lowest crime rate among the three competing states. The amount of park-recreation acreage is also low.

Rivalries among these neighboring states were intense. To lure the Nissan Motor Company to Smyrna, Tennessee, the state provided a $33 million incentive package including job training and site preparation. When indirect incentives are added in, the incentives are $66 million (see

Table 3.5. Tennessee Case—Organization Perspective[a]

	TN	GA	SC
Auto suppliers (1977)	49	38	9
Highway miles (thousands; 1981)	83.5	104.5	62.5
Electricity rate (1982)	6.46	6.28	6.00
Gas rate (1980)	2.53	2.67	2.88
Colleges and universities (1980)	77	76	61
Industrial technology grads (1984/1985)	263	65	94
Dollars per pupil (1981)	2,303	2,329	2,510
Park acreage per capita, ranked (1984)	23	44	27
Doctors per 100,000 (1980)	147.5	135.1	123.5
Median home price (1980)	35,600	36,900	35,100
Crime per 100,000 (1980)	4,311	5,604	5,439

[a]Number in parentheses is the year of the data.

Table 1.1). Table 3.6 presents information for the state perspective, revealing that Tennessee does not have greater state administrative capacity than competitors. Only the areas of financial assistance provided to industry and taxes give Tennessee an edge over competitors.

Although not reflected in our quantitative data, special efforts made by Tennessee's governor and the state legislators also must be considered. Tennessee does not have an overseas office and has less staff devoted to international business, but its governor was well represented in Japan and fully informed about Japanese investment information. In order to recruit Japanese investors to Tennessee, Governor Lamar Alexander made six promotional trips to Japan between 1980 and 1986 and met with the Japanese prime minister three times. He has made efforts to cut administrative red tape in order to facilitate foreign investments and to assure that everything possible was done to maximize the incentives that often make the difference in a company's final decision about where to locate. According to Lamar Alexander, it is important to Tennessee to try harder in order to attract foreign investment since it is a small, insular state, with low incomes and high unemployment rates compared to other states. During the years of Governor Alexander's administration, Tennessee outstripped all other states in the amount of Japanese manufacturing investments. The proinvestment enthusiasm of Tennessee Governor Alexander was also exemplified by a book he wrote, *Friends* (1986), which outlined the reasons so many people and companies from Japan have located in

Table 3.6. Tennessee Case—State Perspective[a]

	TN	GA	SC
Governor's party	DDDRR	RRRRR	RRDDR
House party	ddddd	DDDDD	DDDDD
Senate party	ddddd	DDDDD	DDDDD
Number of government units (1982)	914	1,269	646
International budget ($1000s; 1984)	575	904.5	375.6
Number of staff foreign recruitment (1984)	3	18	7
Number of overseas offices (1986)	0	4	2
Tax incentives (1980)	9	6	9
Financial assistance programs (1980)	8	2	4
Property tax per capita ($, 1980)	158	254.44	160
Total tax per capita ($, 1982)	772	946	842

[a]The time periods for political party affiliation of state governor and state legislatures are five terms preceding the transplant announcing year. These are same for all the cases.

Code for house and senate: D, 75% or more Democratic (strong majority); d, 51–74% Democratic (simple majority); r, 51–74% Republican; R, 75% or more Republican.

Tennessee. It is a public relations effort. He personally presented the book to several hundred Japanese corporations. The state legislators also participated in the statewide effort to bring foreign investment to Tennessee. It is very important to the Nissan plant that every effort made by state government will be backed up in the legislature. The frequent visits, friendly gestures, and warmth all helped to create an atmosphere that attracted Japanese businesses to Tennessee.

Evidence for the class perspective (Table 3.7) indicates that Tennessee has more unionized workers in the labor force, a greater number of work stoppages, a higher wage rate, and a slightly higher welfare expenditure compared with Georgia and South Carolina. Tennessee, Georgia, and South Carolina all have right-to-work laws that virtually guarantee that the unions will remain weak. Governors and mayors openly recruited foreign investors with the promise that the area is union-free. To the foreign investor, the attractions of the South include its special tax breaks and financing opportunities, and what the South's promoters call its probusiness-sometimes read as anti union-environment.

In summary, the most impressive factors in the Tennessee case are the

Table 3.7. Tennessee Case—Class Perspective[a]

	TN	GA	SC
Union (%)	17.5	13.1	6.2
Number of work stoppages	36	23	5
Unemployment	7.1	6.4	8.4
Hourly wage	6.72	6.37	6.18
Per capita income	8,604	8,050	8,960
Weekly workman's compensation benefit	126	115	216
Welfare ($ per capita)	130	129	116
Unemployment benefits (% of weekly wage)	31.8	30.4	34.7

[a]All the data in this table are for 1980.

proinvestment enthusiasm of Tennessee Governor Lamar Alexander and the efforts made by the legislature. The geographic location of Tennessee relative to the existing auto agglomeration in the Midwest and its greater number of auto parts and accessory firms than Georgia and South Carolina should be the other factors that are more attractive to Japanese automakers.

MICHIGAN CASE

Mazda, located in Flat Rock, Michigan, considered ten states in its final list: Michigan, Alabama, Iowa, Kansas, Missouri, Nebraska, North Carolina, Oklahoma, South Carolina, and Tennessee.

Michigan has the availability of auto suppliers (see Table 3.8) and a skilled work force, which has become the basis of an "auto culture." Bachelor (1991) noted the importance put on these factors by Mazda officials. Michigan's economy is tied to durable goods manufacturing. There are sizable clusters of manufacturing industries dedicated to producing specialized industrial infrastructure, networks of suppliers, and complementary industries. This centralization is especially conducive to the Japanese just-in-time auto production process, which certainly enhances Michigan's attractiveness to Japanese automakers. Compared to Michigan, other states have very little auto industry base.

The Michigan site is the only one with an industrial facility currently in place—a vacant Ford Motor company casting facility. Mazda converted it into an automobile assembly plant with extensive modification of the plant and construction of additional structures on the grounds of the facility. The use of existing industrial park facilities and shell buildings

Table 3.8. Michigan Case—Organization Perspective[a]

	MI	AL	IA	KS	MO	NE	OK	SC	TN	NC
Auto suppliers (1982)	447	32	19	9	58	7	28	12	59	39
Highway miles (thousands; 1984)	117.5	87.5	112.4	132.2	118.9	92.0	110.2	63.4	84.1	92.7
Electricity rate (1982)	6.24	5.36	5.57	4.85	6.41	5.74	4.45	6.00	6.46	6.44
Gas rate (1980)	2.87	2.72	2.51	2.24	2.51	2.07	1.96	2.88	2.53	3.22
Colleges and universities (1984)	92	77	59	52	93	21	47	62	75	125
Industrial technology grads (1984/1985)	607	999	193	238	798	86	224	94	263	367
Dollars per pupil (1984)	3,386	2,246	3,578	3,588	3,003	3,520	3,124	2,386	2,290	2,516
Park acreage per capita, ranked (1984)	26	39	13	50	33	6	25	27	23	34
Doctors per 100,000 (1983)	172	136	135	162	175	155	133	141	168	163
Median home price (1980)	39,000	33,900	40,600	37,800	36,700	38,000	35,600	35,100	35,600	36,000
Crime per 100,000 (1984)	6,656	3,902	3,800	4,339	4,297	3,497	4,893	4,663	2,613	4,044

[a]Number in parentheses is the year of the data.

can lead to a considerable reduction in start-up time. This is an important advantage of Flat Rock, Michigan, over other possible sites.

One factor we should mention is that Ford Motor Company played an important role in Mazda's decision to locate in Flat Rock. According to a top official, Mazda's U.S. sales volume was not sufficient to justify building an assembly plant in the United States (see Hill, Indegaard, and Fujita 1989). The agreement between Ford and Mazda that Ford would buy the Ford Probe from Mazda insured the new Mazda plant's capacity (the Ford Probe is designed by Ford, engineered by Mazda, and assembled at Flat Rock). Mazda located in Flat Rock, Michigan, in order to maintain a close relation with Ford and sustain an international division of labor between the companies.

Michigan's state, regional, and local governments' efforts in attracting the automaker to locate in Michigan are also important. Michigan invested a large amount of money in attracting foreign business, and it also has a staff devoted to this subject matter (see Table 3.9). Michigan's governor visited Japan and set an incentive package according to Mazda's needs list. The government at all levels got involved in Mazda's move to Flat Rock, developing an incentive plan that would bring jobs and suppliers along with Mazda. The Flat Rock 100 percent, twelve-year property tax abatement was the largest item in the public incentive package that drew Mazda to Michigan (Bachelor 1991). Table 3.9 shows the difference between Michigan and other competitors regarding number of incentives provided to industry. Michigan's taxes are at the high end, which may be associated with its high education expenditure and high worker compensation payments.

Turning to the class perspective (Table 3.10), comparison among states shows that Michigan has a relative disadvantage in virtually every category. Michigan is a strong union state (indicated by the high percentage of union workers in the labor force and high number of work stoppages), which might deter foreign investors. The high level of wages in manufacturing also means high production costs. However, the higher wage costs in Michigan could reflect higher labor productivity. Japanese automakers are well aware of the importance of an available labor pool, along with auto production skills and attitudes of employees. The high value-added in production allows high labor costs and subsequent economic viability. Since one yardstick in assessing the availability of labor in an area is the level of unemployment within a state, the high level of unemployment in Michigan (see Table 3.10) indicates there is a large pool of surplus workers with the requisite technical skills.

In summary, although Michigan has a strong union force its existing auto culture enhanced Michigan's attractiveness to Japanese automakers. The important role played by Ford Motor Company is another

Table 3.9. Michigan Case—State Perspective[a]

	MI	AL	IA	KS	MO	NE	OK	SC	TN	NC
Governor's party	RRRRD	RRRRR	DDDDD	DDRRR	DRRDD	RRDDR	RRRRR	RRRRR	RRDDD	DRRRR
House party	ddddd	DDDDD	ddrd	rdrrr	ddddd	*	DDddD	DDDDD	ddddd	DDDDD
Senate party	ddddd	DDDDD	ddrd	rrrrr	ddddd	*	DDDDD	ddddd	DDDDD	DDDDD
Number of government units (1982)	2,644	1,019	1,892	3,796	3,118	3,325	2,213	646	914	906
International budget ($1000s; 1984)	1,480.6	600	369.8	82	580	275	500	375.6	575	950
Number of staff foreign recruitment (1984)	21	14	6	3	4.5	5	11	7	3	13
Number of overseas offices (1986)	2	5	1	0	2.5	0	0	2	0	1
Tax incentives (1984)	10	10	8	10	11	5	6	9	9	5
Financial assistance programs (1984)	15	5	3	3	12	5	11	8	5	1
Property tax per capita ($, 1982)	522.9	89.1	436.7	428.5	229.2	448.9	173.6	200.4	195.0	205.9
Total tax per capita ($, 1982)	1,370	806	1,171	1,192	931	1,146	1,123	878	803	911

[a]The time periods for political party affiliation of state governor and state legislatures are five terms preceding the transplant announcing year. These are same for all the cases.
Code for house and senate: D, 75% or more Democratic (strong majority); d, 51–74% Democratic (simple majority); r, 51–74% Republican; R, 75% or more Republican.

Table 3.10. Michigan Case—Class Perspective[a]

	MI	AL	IA	KS	MO	NE	OK	SC	TN	NC
Union (%)	33.9	18.2	20.5	12.0	26.6	16.3	12.9	5.8	17.3	8.9
Number of work stoppages	129	29	41	16	69	11	26	5	36	10
Unemployment	11.2	11.1	7.0	5.2	7.2	4.4	7.0	7.1	8.6	6.7
Hourly wage	12.18	7.97	10.24	9.39	9.31	8.93	9.64	7.28	7.93	7.01
Per capita income	12,518	9,981	12,090	13,319	12,129	12,280	11,745	10,075	10,400	10,758
Weekly workman's compensation benefit	334	184	563	218	212	200	212	269	136	262
Welfare ($ per capita)	446	146	240	189	170	183	215	134	178	152
Unemployment benefits (% of weekly wage)	36.4	31.3	43.7	40.8	27.9	35.5	40.3	32.4	28.5	35.6

[a] All the data in this table are for 1984, except Union (1982) and Work stoppages (1981).

decisive factor in the site selection process that attracted Mazda to Michigan.

ILLINOIS CASE

Four states were involved in the final stage of competition for the Chrysler corporation and Mitsubishi Motors Corporation of Japan joint venture to build small cars in the United States. Two of the states, Ohio and Michigan, already had a Japanese auto plant and were competing for a second plant. Indiana, which was a competitor for Honda, was making its second attempt to attract a transplant.

Table 3.11 presents data related to the organization perspective of location choice. The only advantages that Illinois has over competitors are the number of interstate highway miles, higher education institutions, and physicians per capita. Even if Indiana is considered to be the only "true" competition for Illinois (because both states were without a transplant), one cannot see any special advantages for Illinois.

Data related to the state influences on location decisions (Table 3.12) show Illinois to have substantially more governmental units, a larger budget for international business development, and more overseas offices. Taken together, these factors may indicate that Illinois has both

Table 3.11. Illinois Case—Organization Perspective[a]

	IL	IN	MI	OH
Auto suppliers (1982)	110	126	447	249
Highway miles (thousands; 1985)	134.7	91.4	117.6	113.0
Electricity rate (1982)	6.07	4.66	6.24	5.61
Gas rate (1980)	3.04	2.59	2.87	2.97
Colleges and universities (1985)	163	74	92	141
Industrial technology grads (1984/1985)	594	471	607	204
Dollars per pupil (1985)	3,721	3,209	4,047	3,455
Park acreage per capita, ranked (1984)	28	45	26	43
Doctors per 100,000 (1985)	199	142	174	182
Median home price (1980)	53,900	37,200	39,000	45,100
Crime per 100,000 (1985)	5,303	3,914	6,366	4,187

[a]Number in parentheses is the year of the data.

Table 3.12. Illinois Case—State Perspective[a]

	IL	IN	MI	OH
Governor's party	RRRRR	RRRRR	RRRDD	DRRDD
House party	ddrdd	rrrrr	ddddd	ddddd
Senate party	ddddd	rrrrr	ddddd	rrddd
Number of government units (1982)	6,468	2,866	2,644	3,394
International budget ($1000s; 1984)	2,500	560	1,480.6	1,900
Number of staff foreign recruitment (1984)	31	12	21	39
Number of overseas offices (1986)	5	3	2	3
Tax incentives (1986)	11	11	10	9
Financial assistance programs (1986)	11	15	14	12
Property tax per capita ($, 1982)	425.81	309.98	522.9	328.28
Total tax per capita ($, 1985)	1,474	1,181	1,609	1,331

[a]The time periods for political party affiliation of state governor and state legislatures are five terms preceding the transplant announcing year. These are same for all the cases.

Code for house and senate: D, 75% or more Democratic (strong majority); d, 51–74% Democratic (simple majority); r, 51–74% Republican; R, 75% or more Republican.

greater resources and commitment to attracting foreign investment. This speculation is consistent with the very attractive package of financial incentives that the state of Illinois provided for the Mitsubishi-Chrysler Diamond-Star plant. Some have suggested that the financial incentives were the deciding factor in choosing Illinois (Milward and Newman 1989:217).

Turning to the class factors (Table 3.13), Illinois does not appear to have any advantages compared to competitor states. In fact, all four states in the final competition have relatively strong union climate and social wage expenditures, as reflected in the percentage unionized, number of work stoppages, and spending on welfare, unemployment, and worker compensation. All of this is consistent with the fact that the Mitsubishi-Chrysler plant is unionized, making the factors contained in the class model less relevant when considering the location decision.

In summary, it appears that the main thing that gave Illinois an advantage was an attractive incentive package, a strong educational system, and greater administrative and financial commitment to attracting foreign

Table 3.13. Illinois Case—Class Perspective[a]

	IL	IN	MI	OH
Union (%)	27.5	25.1	33.9	30.0
Number of work stoppages	187	94	129	384
Unemployment	9.1	8.6	11.2	9.4
Hourly wage	10.37	10.71	12.64	11.38
Per capita income	14,728	12,433	14,008	13,219
Weekly workman's compensation benefit	502.36	178.00	358.00	354.00
Welfare ($ per capita)	316	203	446	169
Unemployment benefits (% of weekly wage)	36.3	26.7	36.4	39.3

[a]All the data in this table are for 1986, except Union (1982) and Work stoppages (1981).

corporations. An additional advantage may be found in the fact that two of the three competitor states already had a Japanese transplant, leaving the choice to be Illinois or Indiana.

KENTUCKY CASE

The competition for the Toyota auto transplant investment involves Kentucky, Georgia, Indiana, Kansas, Missouri, and Tennessee as finalists. Among those six finalist states, Tennessee had already attracted Nissan's $745–848 million investment in 1980, and Indiana would be the winner of Fuji-Isuzu's $480–500 million investment in December 1986.

Starting with the organization perspective, Table 3.14 shows that Kentucky has the lowest crime rate and lowest median housing price compared to the other states. It also has the lowest highway mileage and number of higher education institutions. However, those variables are associated with the size of the state. None of the other variables makes Kentucky look different from other states. Surprisingly, the number of auto suppliers is not an important variable.

The only variable in the state perspective that differentiates Kentucky from other states is the low property tax rate (Table 3.15). Although Kentucky is not the highest regarding number of different financial incentives available to industry in general, the state provided a $150 million incentive package for Toyota, which includes purchasing land, preparing the site, highway improvements, and employee training. The training pro-

Table 3.14. Kentucky Case—Organization Perspective[a]

	KY	GA	IN	KS	MO	TN
Auto suppliers (1982)	32	32	126	9	58	59
Highway miles (thousands; 1985)	69.5	106.2	91.4	132.4	119.1	83.8
Electricity rate (1982)	6.38	6.28	4.66	4.85	6.41	6.46
Gas rate (1980)	2.67	2.67	2.59	2.24	2.51	2.53
Colleges and universities (1985)	45	80	74	52	93	80
Industrial technology grads (1984/1985)	198	65	471	238	798	263
Dollars per pupil (1985)	2,513	2,794	3,209	3,744	3,111	2,508
Park acreage per capita, ranked (1984)	40	44	45	50	33	23
Doctors per 100,000 (1985)	146	134	138	162	175	168
Median home price (1980)	34,200	36,900	37,200	37,800	36,700	35,600
Crime per 100,000 (1985)	2,947	5,110	3,914	4,375	4,366	4,167

[a]Number in parentheses is the year of the data.

Table 3.15. Kentucky Case—State Perspective[a]

	KY	GA	IN	KS	MO	TN
Governor's party	DDDDD	RRRRR	RRRRR	DDRRR	DRRDD	RRDDD
House party	DDDDD	DDDDD	drrrr	rdrrr	ddddd	ddddd
Senate party	DDDDd	DDDRD	rdrrr	rrrrr	ddddd	ddddd
Number of government units (1982)	1,242	1,269	2,866	3,796	3,118	914
International budget ($1000s; 1984)	838	904.5	560	82	580	575
Number of staff foreign recruitment (1984)	5.5	18	12	3	10.5	3
Number of overseas offices (1986)	1	4	3	0	2.5	0
Tax incentives (1985)	9	4	11	12	11	9
Financial assistance programs (1985)	8	2	15	3	12	5
Property tax per capita ($, 1982)	150.23	254.44	309.93	428.50	229.16	194.96
Total tax per capita ($, 1982)	855	946	876	1,070	843	772

[a]The time periods for political party affiliation of state governor and state legislatures are five terms preceding the transplant announcing year. These are same for all the cases.

Code for house and senate: D, 75% or more Democratic (strong majority); d, 51–74% Democratic (simple majority); r, 51–74% Republican; R, 75% or more Republican.

gram includes $10 million for a new training facility, to be run jointly by the Cabinet for Human Resources and Toyota, and $33 million over five years for training workers before they are hired and after they are on the job. Education-related incentives also included a Saturday school for Japanese children. The school, to be provided by the University of Kentucky, will teach Japanese language, mathematics, general science, and history. The university, in conjunction with the Kentucky Department of Education, will also provide English classes for Japanese adults and children (*Louisville Courier-Journal*, December 18, 1985).

The class approach works best in the Kentucky case. Our data show that Kentucky has the highest unemployment rate and the lowest per capita individual income level compared with other states (see Table 3.16). The harsh economic conditions usually force the state government to try harder to lure foreign investment into the state. The data also

Table 3.16. Kentucky Case—Class Perspective[a]

	KY	GA	IN	KS	MO	TN
Union (%)	12.0	13.1	25.1	12.0	26.6	17.3
Number of work stoppages	62	35	94	16	69	36
Unemployment	9.5	6.5	7.9	5.0	6.4	8.0
Hourly wage	9.53	8.10	10.71	9.45	9.57	8.29
Per capita income	10,775	12,618	12,433	13,826	13,256	11,263
Weekly workman's compensa-tion benefit	304.8	155.0	178.0	239.0	233.8	168.0
Welfare ($ per capita)	232	190	184	187	186	179
Unemployment benefits (% of weekly wage)	31.6	32.0	26.7	40.8	27.9	28.5

[a]All the data in this table are for 1985, except Union (1982) and Work stoppages (1981).

indicate that Kentucky's public welfare expenditure is the lowest among those six states. Kentucky also has the lowest union representation in its labor force.

Under the pressure of international competition, many state and local governments in the United States have altered their functional priorities— from an emphasis upon regulation and social welfare to an emphasis on government-facilitated economic growth (Hill 1989). Governments want to attract and retain high-value-added activities and foster intraregional linkages among firms in their production systems. State government can raise property taxes or, conversely, can offer locational incentives. Kentucky apparently chose to compete for Toyota with its exceptionally generous financial incentive package. Although usually set at $150 million, some have put the true cost at $350 million, which includes the bond interest payments (Gelsanliter 1992:129).

A final intangible advantage for Kentucky was the aggressive recruiting of its governor, Martha Layne Collins. When a Toyota official was asked why they decided to build their plant in Kentucky, he replied:

> The most decisive factor was the dinner party hosted by Governor Collins in November [1985]. Governor Collins arranged to have many people there— the president of the University of Kentucky, the president of the Kentucky Chamber of Commerce and all these people. Our people thought that here in Kentucky everybody is united to help Toyota. (*Louisville Courier Journal*, October 14, 1986, p. B12)

The governor also apparently made a number of eleventh-hour concessions that won Toyota. The governor would later admit publicly that she was not aware of all of the incentives in Kentucky's package to Toyota (*Lexington Herald-Leader*, July 2, 1986).

INDIANA CASE

In the case of Indiana, the competitors are Illinois and Kentucky. Although Indiana won the Japanese Fuji-Isuzu investment, both Illinois and Kentucky already had a Japanese auto transplant in their jurisdictions (Toyota in Georgetown, Kentucky, and Diamond-Star, a Mitsubishi and Chrysler joint venture in Normal, Illinois). Table 3.17 shows that Indiana has the largest number of auto-related firms compared with Illinois and Kentucky. The utility rates for industry are the lowest in Indiana. Japanese investors are also attracted by the high quality of the engineering school at Purdue University, which graduates one out of every twenty engineers in the United States.

Table 3.17. Indiana Case—Organization Perspective[a]

	IN	IL	KY
Auto suppliers (1982)	126	110	30
Highway miles (thousands; 1986)	91.4	134.8	69.6
Electricity rate (1982)	4.66	6.07	6.38
Gas rate (1980)	2.59	3.04	2.67
Colleges and universities (1986)	76	163	56
Industrial technology grads (1984/1985)	471	594	198
Dollars per pupil (1986)	3,348	3,865	2,541
Park acreage per capita, ranked (1984)	45	28	40
Doctors per 100,000 (1985)	142	199	148
Median home price (1980)	37,200	53,900	34,200
Crime per 100,000 (1986)	3,755	5,546	3,092

[a]Number in parentheses is the year of the data.

Examining state factors (Table 3.18), Indiana does not have any particular advantage over competitors. The state helps foreign investors with tax abatements on buildings or equipment and with funds for infrastructure—water, sewers, and roads. It also gives foreign investors "community loans" (the state gives money to the city or locality, the community lends it to the company, and the company then pays back the loan to the community, which in turn uses it for further economic development); loan guarantees to foreign firms; and research-and-development money. Job-training money is available to send Americans overseas for training on the condition that the jobs remain in Indiana. However, competitor states also provide many similar incentives to business.

Evidence from the class perspective (Table 3.19) indicates that Indiana does not have a particularly stronger or weaker union climate than either of its competitors. The percentage of the labor force in unions is about the same as Illinois, and both states have double the percentage of union workers than Kentucky. Indiana has fewer work stoppages than Illinois, and has higher welfare expenditures than its competitors. The strongest probusiness factors in Indiana are the very low rate of worker compensation benefits and the lower unemployment benefits.

Indiana's attractiveness to Fuji-Isuzu was probably due to the efforts of its lieutenant governor, to the value of the financial incentive package, and to the fact that it was the last piece in the puzzle of six contiguous states, each with an auto transplant. Lieutenant Governor John M. Mutz, head of the Indiana Department of Commerce, was the lead negotiator

Table 3.18. Indiana Case—State Perspective[a]

	IN	IL	KY
Governor's party	RRRRR	DDDDD	DDDDD
House party	rrrrr	ddrdd	DDDDD
Senate party	drrrr	ddddd	DDDDd
Number of government units (1982)	2,866	6,468	1,242
International budget ($1000s; 1984)	560	2,500	838
Number of staff foreign recruitment (1984)	12	31	5.5
Number of overseas offices (1986)	3	5	1
Tax incentives (1986)	11	11	8
Financial assistance programs (1986)	15	11	12
Property tax per capita ($, 1982)	309.98	425.81	150.23
Total tax per capita ($, 1986)	1,227	1,547	1,104

[a]The time periods for political party affiliation of state governor and state legislatures are five terms preceding the transplant announcing year. These are same for all the cases.

Code for house and senate: D, 75% or more Democratic (strong majority); d, 51–74% Democratic (simple majority); r, 51–74% Republican; R, 75% or more Republican.

Table 3.19. Indiana Case—Class Perspective[a]

	IN	IL	KY
Union (%)	25.1	27.5	12.0
Number of work stoppages	94	187	62
Unemployment	6.7	8.1	9.3
Hourly wage	10.81	10.67	9.86
Per capita income	13,109	15,467	11,227
Weekly workman's compensation benefit	178.00	511.81	316.54
Welfare ($ per capita)	203	316	249
Unemployment benefits (% of weekly wage)	26.7	36.3	31.6

[a]All the data in this table are for 1986, except Union (1982) and Work stoppages (1981).

with the Japanese on the state's incentive package. He made several trips to Japan during the months when Fuji and Isuzu were deciding where to build their first joint venture in the United States. Indiana's direct incentive payments to lure Fuji-Isuzu to build a Subaru-Isuzu plant totaled $83 million. However, the tax credits and abatements, utility rate reductions, and other direct benefits may cost the state more than $260 million. Fuji-Isuzu also got a land deal—the Indiana Employment Development Commission (an independent agency) bought and developed the land and leased it for a nominal amount to a Japanese company.

Indiana's international development agency, a branch of the State Department of Commerce, has three foreign offices representing Indiana's interests in Tokyo, Brussels, and London. The state's branch office in Tokyo is very skillful in recruiting Japanese investors. It had handled 325 new foreign investments or expansions from 1981 to 1985. The total expenditure for attracting foreign investment for fiscal year 1986 was $304,100, or 45 percent of the state's total international appropriation (National Association of State Development Agencies).

The location of the Subaru-Isuzu plant in Indiana creates an impressive regional base for an automobile industry composed of six large assembly plants and hundreds of suppliers. The proximity of SIA in Indiana to the Mazda plant in Michigan, Honda in Ohio, Toyota in Kentucky, Nissan in Tennessee, and Mitsubishi-Chrysler in Illinois makes it especially attractive to Japanese auto suppliers, who are trying to take advantage of the Japanese preference for doing business with companies from their own country.

SUMMARY OF FINDINGS AND REGRESSION ANALYSIS

The case by case comparisons of states that were in competition for transplants provides some answers to the question of why they located where they did. States that were the winners differed from competitors on several characteristics associated with the organization and state perspectives of industrial location. The class model is noteworthy because of its failure to distinguish winner and competitor states, a point we will return to shortly.

1. Four of the six states that attracted a transplant (Ohio, Indiana, Michigan, and Tennessee) had a stronger auto supplier infrastructure than did their competitors. A fifth winner state, Illinois, also had a large number of suppliers, but not more than the competitor states of Michigan and Ohio, which already had transplants. Thus, the Illinois case is consis-

tent with the other four cases, providing strong evidence that the auto supplier infrastructure was an important determinant of the location decisions made by the Japanese firms.

2.   Although no single factor in the state perspective provided consistent evidence across the six cases, there is general evidence that states with administrative capacity and resources to pursue foreign investment, and with active and aggressive chief executives, were most often the states chosen as sites for transplants. When this evidence is combined with the very attractive financial incentive packages developed by winner states, we can conclude that the state model of industrial location received strong support from our data. A caveat to this generalization is that we do not have comparative data on the incentive packages developed by the competitor states and therefore do not know if their offers were more substantial than the winner states. However, some Japanese corporate officials have suggested that the details of incentives are discussed only after they decide on a state. The incentives can serve to cancel out disadvantages and to make two sites appear equally attractive (*Louisville Courier-Journal*, October 14, 1986, p. B12).

3.   Findings from the class model indicate that Japanese firms did not try to avoid states that had the potential of a militant, prounion labor force, and provided a more generous social wage in the form of welfare benefits, unemployment benefits, and worker's compensation. This is surprising, in view of the fact that executives from most of the auto transplants were forthright about their opposition to labor unions. Our speculation about the weakness of the class model is that by the mid-1980s organized labor had been weakened and was already under great pressure from management about wage concessions, work rules, and fringe benefits. Even the unionized Japanese auto plants at Mazda, Mitsubishi, and NUMMI in California provided examples of less militant unions working closely with management to increase productivity through major changes in work rules. In short, a weakened and less militant labor movement made it possible for Japanese firms to concentrate on factors other than labor militancy when making their location decision: hence the explanatory strength of the organization and state models over the class model.

Based on these findings, we selected four variables from each of the three perspectives that are most likely (on empirical or theoretical grounds) to be determinants of the location decision. For each perspective (organization, state, and class) we regress two dichotomous variables on the four variables defined as determinants of the location decision. The first dichotomous variable divides all states in the United States into winner plus competitor states, and all other states. This dichotomous variable reflects an early stage in the decision process, when the Japanese firms were trying to select a region in which to locate or were identifying a number of states that might be desirable locations. The second dichotomous variable is winner versus competitor states, reflecting the final stage in the site selection process.

This regression analysis will permit us to identify the relative importance of selected variables in the organization, state, and class perspectives, and to see if the variables that are important differ at the two decision stages. For example, we know from the analysis done earlier in this chapter that the number of auto supplier firms was an important variable separating winner from competitor states. With the regression analysis, we will learn if the number of auto supplier firms is important when we simultaneously consider the influence of three other variables, such as the number of industrial technology graduates, the median price of homes, and the crime rate. We will also learn if the auto supplier variable was important in separating all winner and competitor states from all other states, leading to the conclusion that it is an important factor in the early decision by Japanese firms and in the final decision. However, because of the small number of cases (i.e., states) available for this analysis, the regression results should be viewed as provisional and exploratory.

Table 3.20 contains a summary of the regression analysis for the three

Table 3.20. Regression Analysis for Organization, State, and Class Perspectives

Variable	Winner and competitor vs. other states	Winner vs. competitor states
Organization perspective		
Auto suppliers	−.415***	−.801***
Industrial technology grads	−.078	.168
Median home price	.318*	−.140
Crime rate	−.107	.600*
R^2	.28	.51
State perspective		
International budget	−.496**	−.165
Staff in foreign recruitment	.148	−.191
Total tax per capita	.373**	.165
Incentive programs	.082	−.441
R^2	.20	.41
Class perspective		
Unemployment rate	−.050	−.511*
Work stoppages	−.081	−.405
Welfare per capita	.108	.155
Unemployment benefits	.184	−.189
R^2	.06	.49

*$p < .10.$ **$p < .05.$ ***$p < .01.$

perspectives on location decisions. Starting with the organization perspective, we can see that the number of auto supplier firms is an important factor separating states at both an early stage in the location decision and at the final stage. This suggests that the auto executives making the site selection decision used the supplier infrastructure to identify the set of acceptable sites (winner and competitor states) with whom they would begin negotiations, and to select the final site (winner vs. competitor states). The median price of homes also distinguished states at an early stage in the decision process, and the crime rate distinguished states at the final decision stage. These variables are indicative of cost of living and quality of life in a state, but their statistical significance is not very strong.

Results from the state perspective indicate that the size of a state's budget for international business development and a state's total taxes per capita were related to the early stage in the location decision. States with a larger international budget and lower per capita taxes were more likely to be states that were considered as possible site locations. None of the variables in the state perspective were statistically significant in separating winner from competitor states, although the winner states had larger international budgets, more staff for foreign recruitment, and more business incentive programs.

Only one variable from the class perspective distinguished states in the regression analysis. Winner states had significantly higher unemployment rates than did competitor states. None of the class variables was related to the status of a state (winner/competitor vs. other) at the early stage in the decision process.

We did one more regression analysis in which we combined five variables from the three perspectives: auto suppliers, industrial technology graduates, international budget, total taxes, and level of unemployment benefits. This will permit us to see if variables of one perspective are more important than others. Table 3.21 presents the results of this final regression, which indicate that the number of auto supplier firms and per capita

Table 3.21. Regression Analysis for Combined Variables from Three Perspectives

Variable	Winner and competitor vs. other states	Winner vs. competitor states
Auto suppliers	−.385**	−.775**
Industrial technology grads	−.010	.272
International budget	−.096	−.415
Total tax per capita	.326**	.712**
Unemployment benefits	.110	−.133
R^2	.30	.54

**$p < .10$.

taxes were significantly related to a state's status at the early stage and final stage of the site location decision process. One of these variables is from the organization perspective and one is from the state perspective. These findings are consistent with the results from the case analysis earlier in this chapter, and with the regression analysis of four variables from each perspective. The results of this combined regression should be viewed as very tentative, because we are dealing with very few cases relative to the predictor variables, especially at the final stage in the decision process.

CONCLUSION

Our answer to the question of *why* the transplants selected the six states in the Midwest corridor is that the Japanese apparently placed great emphasis on the infrastructure of auto suppliers in making their site selection decisions. This infrastructure was needed as the basis of their just-in-time approach to handling inventory, and provided the necessary core firms until such time that Japanese auto supplier firms could be established in each state. None of the other traditional location theory variables from the organization perspective consistently differentiated states in the case analysis and regression analysis. While some of these variables may still be important, they did not override the consistent importance of auto supplier infrastructure.

Variables from the state perspective that reflected a state's capacity for dealing with international recruitment also revealed a coherent theoretical pattern, even though the same variables did not show their importance throughout the case and regression analyses. These variables gain greater significance in combination with many of the qualitative factors that were considered in the case analysis. For example, the existence of an aggressive governor, a supportive state legislature, and an attractive incentive package may be the basis for a state having a substantial international development budget and the staff needed to implement that budget. Administrative capacity and resources to pursue foreign investment are but quantitative indicators of the qualitative commitments of states' chief executives.

Variables from the class perspective related to prounion climate and a higher social wage did not reveal a pattern of differentiating states at any stage of the site selection decision. Many of these variables have been a part of traditional location theory, but they did not have appreciable influence on the decisions of the transplants. It may be that the importance of traditional business/economic factors influencing location decisions are declining relative to the increasing influence of an activist local state.

Chapter 4

Selling Growth to Small-Town America: Media Images

City dwellers in the antebellum Middle West lived in the midst of sustained excitement about urban growth... .For men at the top, there was little distinction between urban growth and personal success in banking, trade, transportation, and land speculation. Further down the social ladder, the chance for "participation in the thriving cities gave even the losers in the free-for-all a vicarious victory."

—Carl Abbott, *Boosters and Businessmen*

As this chapter was being written, my hometown newspaper had a front-page headline: "Frankfort Weighs Incentive Package for Manufacturing Plant." The story is, by now, a familiar one. Frankfort, a town of 14,754 residents, has a chance to get a new manufacturing company that will bring 125 new jobs which will pay seven to twelve dollars an hour. The Ann Arbor, Michigan, company is interested in a site in Frankfort, but without the incentive package it will take its $40 million and build elsewhere. The incentive package includes $1.3 million in infrastructure improvements and job training, ten-year tax abatements for $30 million worth of new plant and equipment, and about $900,000 to help the company's start-up costs. In addition, the company will get an interest-free $5 million loan, which will be paid by the company's future taxes (a device called tax increment financing, where taxes on new development are used for further economic development and may not be used for schools, roads, public welfare, or other government activities). The main person speaking in this newspaper story is the president of the County Economic Advancement Foundation.

This is the way most communities learn about new economic development projects. The people of Frankfort and Clinton County will learn about the details of this project, the pros and cons, through their local

77

newspapers. Opinions about whether it is a good or bad idea will be shaped largely by the way the newspapers choose to frame the issue.

In this chapter we examine newspaper coverage of the transplant projects in three states: Tennessee, Kentucky, and Indiana. We examine coverage devoted to transplants by six newspapers—one local paper and one state paper from each of the states. The period of coverage is thirteen months, beginning with the first newspaper story that mentioned the possibility of a Japanese auto plant moving to their state or city.

The purpose of this analysis is to see how newspapers deal with the complex task of trying to assess the potential costs and benefits of the projects. State government leaders who have negotiated with Japanese automobile executives have done so believing that the new plants will produce substantial economic benefits for the community. However, there is the possibility of opposition from environmentalists, organized labor, and concerned taxpayers who see the plant as imposing a cost on them. Given this great potential for public controversy and community conflict, what has been the role of local newspapers in their state's economic development activities? How have they presented the state government's use of public monies to attract foreign automobile manufacturers? Do they seek to shape public awareness and public opinion? If so, do they take a critical, independent stance or do they function as part of a legitimation process that supports the state government's actions?

This chapter will examine these questions by analyzing the amount and type of newspaper coverage of the establishment of the Subaru-Isuzu, Toyota, and Nissan projects provided by the *Lafayette Journal and Courier* (local newspaper), *Indianapolis Star* (state paper), *Lexington Herald-Leader* (local paper), *Louisville Courier-Journal* (state paper), *Murfreesboro Daily News Journal* (local paper), and the *Nashville Tennessean* (state paper). We begin by assuming that newspapers are the principal source of information for citizens about the general issues of growth and development, and about specific efforts by state governments to use economic incentives to attract Japanese auto plants. We expect that local newspapers' portrayals of the auto plant project will reflect the structure of community influence, be it the views of economic and political elites, diverse interest groups, or citizen participation in local issues. We further expect that state newspapers will differ from their local counterparts in that they will concentrate mainly on the benefits of growth.

NEWSPAPERS AND THE POLITICS OF GROWTH

There are sharply contrasting views of the role of newspapers in contemporary society (see, e.g., Altschull 1984; Rachlin 1988; Schudson 1978;

Tuchman 1978). One perspective emphasizes the news media's commitment to the values of objectivity and impartiality. Newspapers do not reflect the views of any particular segment of society, but provide a balance of information that enables the public to develop informed opinions. The activities of the news media are linked to democratic principles through maintaining an open marketplace of ideas and satisfying the public's need to know. Based on this perspective, we would expect newspapers to provide a diversity of points of view and information on the advantages and disadvantages of bringing an auto transplant to their area.

A second perspective on newspapers questions their alleged neutrality and objectivity, stressing instead their strong business interests and their bias toward economic growth (Logan and Molotch 1987). A newspaper has a direct interest in growth because it is a business whose financial status is related to the size of the local community and its aggregate growth (Molotch 1976). As a city expands, a newspaper, which benefits primarily from increased ad lines and circulation, will be able to increase its customers, revenues, and profits. National newspapers have strong institutional ties to dominant centers of power and use their influence to legitimize existing political and economic structures (Drier 1982). At the local level, newspapers have been found to be central participants in networks of interlocked organizations and elites (Perrucci and Pilisuk 1970; Perrucci and Lewis 1989). Based on this perspective, we would expect newspapers to provide a narrow range of positive views of the transplant project.

The validity of either of these perspectives can be determined by examining how newspapers shape the way that readers will think about the transplants. How newspapers shape the reality of the transplants can occur along three dimensions. The first dimension involves how newspapers deal with the potential legal and political problems that can arise from the state's initiative to become actively and directly involved in a "new partnership" with a private corporation. The transplant project represents a break with the old way of encouraging economic development and, as such, has the potential to generate opposition or support. The issues created by the actions of the state are ideological ("The state has no business funding private corporations"), legal ("Does the state constitution permit land to be acquired and used for a private purpose?"), and political ("Spending all that money is not going to help the average person in our town"). The ideological issue is probably the least contentious, given the long history of state and local governments' involvement in working with business to stimulate economic growth. The other two issues, however, have the potential for conflict, and thus the role of local newspapers in presenting these issues is important.

The second dimension concerns who speaks on the transplant topic. To be given space to express opinions on the transplant is to be given the standing of a consequential actor, or someone whose ideas should be taken into consideration by others. Newspapers make choices about the persons or organizations that are allowed to speak on the topic. Thus, newspapers can cover a community issue in a way that allows persons / organizations to speak who come from many institutional areas of the community, or from few areas. They can project an image of broad support for a project or one of competing interest groups with different views of what is best for the community. In addition, issues can be framed in a way that invites citizen involvement (e.g., call for public meetings, or sponsor "Express Yourself" phone-ins) or emphasizes the expertise of specialists or professionals to shape public opinion. We might think of this dimension as the populist-elitist dimension.

The third dimension along which newspapers shape the reality of the transplants is the cost-benefit continuum of consequences connected with the transplant. Newspapers can choose to emphasize the benefits of growth to a community and the responsibility of government to promote the growth process. Such an emphasis would give central attention to the efforts of local political and business leaders trying to improve employment and income through the pursuit of new employers or expansion of existing businesses. In contrast, newspapers can choose to focus on the costs of growth, such as environmental impact and the possible changes in the quality of life for residents. The particular balance of coverage between costs and benefits can influence how the community reacts to the transplant project.

Thus, we analyze newspaper coverage in terms of legitimizing incentives, the persons and organizations who are called upon to speak through the newspaper, and the coverage of topics in the paper that stress the costs or benefits of the transplant project. In addition, we assess the amount of space provided to the transplant topic and whether that coverage is positive or negative toward the transplant.

The unit of analysis in this chapter is the newspaper clippings obtained from six newspapers. We collected every item in the Kentucky papers that mentioned Toyota; every item in the Tennessee papers that mentioned Nissan; and every item in the Indiana papers that mentioned Subaru-Isuzu. The clippings were collected for a thirteen-month period from each newspaper, starting with the first story on the transplants. The numbers of clippings analyzed are as follows: 139 from the *Louisville Courier-Journal* and 60 from the *Lexington Herald-Leader* from December 1985 through December 1986; 236 from the *Lafayette Journal and Courier* and 32 from the *Indianapolis Star*, obtained from December 1986 through December 1987; and 115 from the *Murfreesboro Daily News Journal* and 43 from the *Nashville*

Tennessean, obtained from September 1980 through September 1981. The items are primarily news stories (86 to 95 percent) with the remainder being editorials and letters to the editor.

LEGITIMIZING INCENTIVES FOR CORPORATISM

Corporatism, as discussed in Chapter 1, involves an activist local state working with the business class to provide millions of dollars of public funds to foreign firms as an incentive to locate plants in their state. The ideology of corporatism stresses a new partnership between local government and private corporations to advance common interests in economic growth. The corporatist project, embodied by the transplants, represents a departure from established or traditional ways of fostering economic development. As noted in Chapter 2, traditional ways of fostering development involved modest (by current standards) financial incentives of tax relief, or nonfinancial incentives of providing information or assisting with regulatory problems or worker training. In contrast, the corporatist project involves multi–hundred million dollar agreements of direct, in-advance expenditures as well as indirect costs related to interest on revenue bonds for land acquisition.

The corporatist project also involves a new relationship between government and private corporations that is not yet justified or legitimized in the institutional arrangements that facilitated past government-business relationships. For example, the state constitution in Indiana forbids the state to acquire land that is to be given to a private corporation. Unless the old rules governing how government and private corporations do business are changed, the state's plan to provide land to the transplant is going to be viewed as unconstitutional. Another potential problem with the corporatist project is a political one. Is the public at large, or are the elected officials representing that public, prepared to accept the spending of tens of millions in tax dollars on the promise that the state will recover its investment without harming the public good?

Unless the legal and political hurdles facing the corporatist project can be overcome or circumvented, it will not be possible to create the new institutional arrangements that are required to fund and support the transplants. New institutional guidelines are essential, because the transplant project is just the first step in a new relationship between state and local governments and private corporations. The incentive package for a particular Japanese auto firm will be followed by hundreds of smaller supplier firms that will need land, tax abatements, relief from regulatory restrictions, and the like. Moreover, each of these entities may be thinking about future expansion of operations, and will thus have a need for its earlier arrangements and agreements to be "institutionalized." That means that the new way of doing government-corporation business will be viewed as legitimate in both a legal and normative sense. This is what was discussed in Chapter 2 as an emerging social structure of accumulation to solve the problems that limit capital accumulation.

Legal Legitimacy. The first thirteen months of coverage of the Nissan auto plant by two newspapers in Tennessee contains no mention of the legal or constitutional basis for the state's decision to provide financial incentives to the auto firm. The *Nashville Tennessean* contained 5 stories about the incentive package from a total of 43 stories (12 percent). The *Murfreesboro Daily News Journal* published 115 auto plant stories during the same period, with 11 stories (10 percent) concerned with incentives. The concern of the stories is the amount of the incentives and not the legal right of the state to do what it is doing to assist private corporations.

The absence of discussion of the legal basis of incentives in Tennessee's newspapers is consistent with a scholarly treatment of the subject. Green (1990) provides a clear and concise discussion of the use of incentives to bring the Japanese auto plants to the six states in the Midwest corridor. Green informs us that states use three types of inducements to private industry: "interest subsidies in the form of direct loans, loan guarantees, or industrial development bonds" as a way of providing low-cost capital; "production input subsidies. . .for land acquisition, plant site preparation and construction, equipment purchases, and worker training"; and "tax subsidies in the form of. . .tax exemptions" (p. 54). Green maintains that interest and production subsidies are the most constitutionally troublesome, because they directly challenge constitutional provisions designed to limit a state from financing private corporations.

Constitutional questions were not raised in Tennessee because Rutherford County sold $700 million in development bonds to Nissan to finance the purchase and development of a site and construction of the Nissan plant. Nissan pays rent on the facility and the rent is used to pay off the bonds by the year 2011. At that time Nissan will purchase the plant for a nominal amount of money. Thus, Tennessee finances and owns the auto facility and rents it to Nissan.

In the case of Indiana, there is a mixture of government ownership of the land and Fuji-Isuzu ownership of the plant (Green 1990:64). The Japanese firms constructed the plant with private financing, and the state financed the purchase and development of the plant site, and leased it to Fuji-Isuzu for one hundred dollars a year. The state incentive package could have been constitutionally challenged on two grounds: (1) Were state funds being used to serve a public purpose, as prescribed by the constitution? (2) Was the state incurring debt to purchase the land for the auto plant, which was prohibited by the constitution?

The second story on the transplant to appear in the *Lafayette Journal and Courier* mentioned the constitutional issue, and how it was circumvented. The December 4, 1986 front-page story ("Auto Plant: A Plan Comes Together"), described the issue:

> The state can't buy the land outright because it can't afford to: the constitution prohibits deficit financing. The constitution also prevents giving away land or issuing bonds to pay for financial incentive programs. (p. A1)

Constitutional prohibitions were circumvented by the creation of a nonprofit corporation that would buy the land and lease it to Fuji-Isuzu at a nominal cost for six years, and then transfer it to the automakers at no additional cost. The state's director of industrial development for the Indiana Department of Commerce states that they worked closely with the attorney general's office "to ensure that the ownership and purchase of the land met all constitutional requirements."

The December 4 *Lafayette Journal and Courier* account reported that no information was provided about the nonprofit corporation that acquired and leased the land to Fuji-Isuzu. On December 27, the paper published a thirty-two-page, five-column special report on Fuji-Isuzu, covering a chronology of events leading to the transplant, key state and local leaders who shaped the plan, impacts on the community, use of incentives, jobs, wages, unions, and settling Japanese families in the community. Four lines in one column of this issue state: "The Indiana Employment Development Commission (IEDC) has approved a resolution to borrow $10 million from Lafayette National Bank and Bank One Lafayette to buy 873 acres of land for the Fuji-Isuzu plant" (p. D1).

The question of the constitutionality of the state's incentive package surfaced one more time in the *Lafayette Journal and Courier*, on February 15, 1987. The headline at the top of the page stated: "Auto Plant Dredges Up Ill Will." The center of the page has a 5"×6" graphic containing American and Japanese flags and two hands clasped in friendship. Four stories surround the graphic, two opposed to incentives and two that support the transplant project and the use of incentives. The two anti-incentive stories are about Donald W. Mantooth, former candidate for Mayor of Indianapolis, unsuccessful candidate for the Democratic nomination for governor, and nominee for the Indiana house of representatives. Mantooth is circulating a petition calling on state legislators to vote against the $86 million incentive package to Fuji-Isuzu. One story opens: "The state is thumbing its nose at the constitution by paving the way for the Subaru-Isuzu Automotive plant." The proincentive/transplant stories feature two state officials from the Indiana Department of Commerce who were involved in negotiating the incentive package.

The Indiana case suggests that the constitutional question was avoided because the state followed the letter of the law, but did not necessarily follow its spirit. The nonprofit Indiana Employment Development Commission was acting as an agent of the state, but it was legally a separate entity. Clearly, the two newspapers covering the transplant story show little interest in questioning the legal standing of incentives.

Kentucky is also a case of mixed ownership and financing, with Toyota as owner of the improved site, which the state purchased from the sale of bonds and delivered to Toyota, and with the plant construction jointly financed by the state and Toyota (Green 1990:66). The Kentucky-Toyota financing agreement required legislation, and the bill drafted in the Kentucky Senate for financing economic development projects ran into constitutional challenges. A circuit court judge ruled that the actions of the state were constitutional, and the decision was appealed to the Kentucky Supreme Court, which ruled four to three in favor of the state.

The existence of the legal challenge to the incentive made the topic visible in the local and state newspapers of Kentucky. The first newspaper story announcing that Toyota had selected Tennessee as the site for their auto plant was on December 12, 1985. On January 24, 1986 the *Louisville Courier-Journal* had a page one story: "State's plan to give Toyota land may be unconstitutional." The story cites the opinions of the Attorney General, several state legislators, and several attorneys to the effect that it would be unconstitutional for the state to provide free land to Toyota. Representatives of the governor's office indicated that the question of "land giveaway" was considered early in negotiations and judged to be doable. They also indicated that if there were constitutional problems, the land could be leased to Toyota.

On January 25, 1986, another front-page story in the same paper ("Senate Passes Toyota Resolution after Debate") reports a thirty-one to two vote in the state senate on a resolution pledging to allocate the money needed for the state to honor Governor Collins's commitments to Toyota. In the debate on the resolution, several senators indicate that state law prohibits giving or leasing land for less that fair market value. The discussion of constitutional issues is only a fragment of a larger story on the incentive package.

The question of constitutionality would be mentioned again in a news story on February 25, 1986 ("2 Collins Aides Sent to Wrap Up Toyota Details"), devoting 8 lines to it in a 224-line story. The topic would not appear again until May 8, 1986 ("State Files Test Suit on Toyota"), reporting a "friendly lawsuit" filed by the governor and attorney general seeking a ruling on the constitutionality of the state's plans for financing the

Toyota project. This marked the beginning of a legal process that would proceed to a circuit court and the state supreme court, and culminate in a four to three decision that Governor Collins's administration "acted legally in offering millions of dollars worth of land and other incentives to lure Toyota Motor Co. to Georgetown" (*Lexington Herald-Leader*, June 12, 1987, p. 1). Writing for the majority, Justice Donald C. Wintersheimer stated:

> In this instance, the legislature, working in conjunction with the executive, determined that it was proper to attempt to alleviate unemployment and develop economic strength in the state through the financing of an industrial development project. . .which constitutes the effectuation of a proper public purpose.
> . . .The specific language of Section 177 [of the constitution] involved is that the credit of the commonwealth shall not be given, pledged or loaned to any individual company or corporation.. . .
> However, as long as the expenditure of public money has as its purpose the effectuation of a valid public purpose, Section 117 is not offended even in situations where the conveyance occurs without consideration.. . .
> The obligation of Toyota to pay taxes in the future is significantly more than the obligation of any taxpayer in the semi-rural tract in question. The new taxes are incremental in nature and would not exist but for the establishment of the industrial complex. In no sense of the word is the conveyance of the project site a donation to a private corporation as prohibited by Section 117. (p. 1)

In a dissenting opinion, Justice Charles W. Leibson stated:

> We have succumbed to powerful non-judicial arguments advanced to uphold this legislation in the face of constitutional challenge. . . .Pressure on the judiciary to find some way around the constitution in the name of political expediency has proved to be overwhelming.
> . . .Because the prospect of incremental taxes is not payment in any direct sense of the word, the conveyance of the project site is a "donation" to a private corporation prohibited by Section 177.
> . . .The legislative declaration of a public purpose standing alone is not enough to avoid our constitutional prohibition against public grants to a private person or corporation, no matter how powerful the arguments that the public will benefit from the business conducted by the private enterprise. (p. 1)

Aside from the legal arguments supporting and opposing the constitutionality of the incentive package, it is probably safe to say that the state newspapers did not seem eager to make the legal legitimacy of the incentives an issue in the public's mind. During an almost five-month period preceding the state's friendly lawsuit, Kentucky newspapers mentioned the constitutionality question three times. The newspapers could have made the legality of incentives a highly visible issue, given the large number of opponents to the incentives to be found among the state's attorneys and legislators, to say nothing of opponents from labor, environmental groups, and the small-business sector.

Political Legitimacy. The matter of political legitimacy focuses on the question of who benefits from the spending of millions of dollars of public funds for the transplant project. It is much broader than the matter of legal legitimacy and it invites the participation of a wider array of interest groups and the public at large to offer their views on the incentive package and the transplant project. The usual focus of attention in the struggle for political legitimacy starts with questions of how much the state is going to spend on the project, how it is going to be spent, and how long it will take to get back the money.

These are difficult questions under the best of circumstances, that is, when there is detailed financial information about the incentive package. But the question of how much the state is going to spend is a moving target. It grows and declines with some frequency in newspaper accounts, leaving even those interested in the topic somewhat befuddled:

> Although the incentive package was negotiated more than 10 months ago and approved by the General Assembly last spring, some legislators said they still are confused about some specifics.. . .Representative Carl Nett, D-Louisville summed up what seemed to be universal frustration about the way numbers have been interpreted. "We're all just talking theory anyway," he said, "There's no way we'll get all these numbers figured out for at least 10 years." (*Louisville Courier-Journal*, October 24, 1986, p. B1)

Part of the problem is due to the documents that are provided by the state to describe the agreements between state and local governments and the auto plant. For example, at one extreme is the Kentucky-Toyota agreement, an eight-page document signed on February 25, 1986, by Shoichiro Toyoda, president of Toyota Motor Corporation, and Martha Layne Collins, governor of Kentucky. The document contains very few specifics, and it would not be possible to find the state's $125 million in incentives in the document. As Green (1990) has noted, the details of agreements on incentives are usually contained in letters between the auto company and state and local officials, and not in the formal agreement.

However, the Indiana–Fuji-Isuzu agreement is the exception, and is at the other extreme from the Kentucky-Toyota agreement document. Indiana provided a twenty-one-page Memorandum of Understanding, signed on December 1, 1986, by John M. Mutz, lieutenant governor of Indiana, Akira Soejima, senior managing director of Fuji Heavy Industries, and

Yasuo Yamamoto, managing director of Isuzu Motors. The document provides unusual detail of the things the state will do, and their cost, in regard to acquisition of land, site preparation, roadway improvements, railway lines, water-sanitary lines, gas and electricity, recruitment, screening, and training of work force, and much more.

The point of this contrast between the Kentucky and Indiana documents regarding agreements with auto firms is that in the absence of detailed information in the public record, there will be greater opportunity for confusion and conflict regarding the costs and benefits. In addition to the need for better information on the direct costs of incentives, there should be a full accounting of indirect costs, such as property tax abatements, tax credits, and interest on bond issues. Information on indirect incentives is rarely presented in newspaper coverage of the transplant projects, leading to the impression that newspapers may wish to understate the cost of incentives and thereby minimize public controversy about incentives.

In the remainder of this chapter we examine newspaper coverage of the transplants, and the way in which this coverage contributes to, or undermines, the political legitimacy of the corporatist project.

WHO SPEAKS ON THE TRANSPLANTS?

Table 4.1 contains a summary of all the persons and organizations expressing views on the transplants in each of the six newspapers. Those who are mentioned in the news items are classified into three sectors: social sector, business and industry, and elected leaders and government agency officials. It can be seen from Table 4.1 that the largest percentages of persons and organizations mentioned are elected leaders and agency officials, ranging from 41 percent of all mentions in the local Kentucky paper to 66 percent of all mentions in the state Tennessee paper. The next largest group of persons and organizations is from the business and industry sector, ranging from a low of 16 percent in the state Kentucky paper, to 38 percent in the state Indiana newspaper. The social sector of labor, education, religion, and social agencies / organizations received the fewest opportunities to have their views on the transplants represented.

What these data indicate is that public discussion of the transplant project in local and state newspapers is dominated by representatives of government, both local and state, and by representatives of the business community. These are the persons and organizations with the greatest vested interest in the project, and those most likely to reap economic benefits. They are the governors, mayors, and economic development

Table 4.1. Persons/Organizations from Different Community Sectors Mentioned in News Accounts

Community sector	Indiana newspapers				Kentucky newspapers				Tennessee newspapers			
	Local		State		Local		State		Local		State	
	N	%	N	%	N	%	N	%	N	%	N	%
Sector 1: Social sector												
Labor	6	1.0	6	7.0	23	15.3	164	20.0	15	4.3	1	0.8
Education	60	9.8	9	10.6	12	8.0	40	4.9	15	4.3	2	1.6
Religion	1	0.2	2	2.3	0	—	0	—	0	—	0	—
Social agencies / organizations	15	2.4	0	—	0	—	3	0.4	0	—	0	—
Subtotal		13.4		19.9		23.3		25.3		8.6		2.4
Sector 2: Business and industry												
Business-industry	56	9.2	17	20.0	8	5.3	21	2.6	78	22.6	30	24.2
Professionals (e.g., attorneys)	47	7.7	6	7.0	19	12.7	85	10.4	12	3.5	3	2.4
Associations (e.g., Chamber of Commerce)	117	19.1	9	10.6	17	11.3	25	3.0	6	1.7	6	4.8
Subtotal		36.0		37.6		29.3		16.0		27.8		31.4
Sector 3: Elected leaders and agency officials												
Local	146	23.9	5	5.9	19	12.7	82	10.0	75	21.7	25	20.2
State	146	23.9	30	35.3	34	22.7	227	27.7	115	33.3	56	45.2
National	14	2.3	1	1.0	8	5.3	93	11.3	16	4.6	1	0.8
Subtotal		50.1		42.2		40.7		49.0		59.6		66.2
Other	4	0.6			10	6.7	81	9.9	13	3.8		
Totals	612	100.1	85	99.7	150	100	821	100.2	345	99.8	124	100

officials who negotiated the terms of incentive packages with the Japanese auto firms. They are the state legislators who argued and voted for providing state funds for the transplants. They are the real estate speculators and developers who will benefit from growing demand for land and buildings. They are the landlords and bankers who hope to serve a growing population. They are the business leaders who see growth as a win-win situation, emphasizing the advantages of a $500 million plant, two thousand new jobs, $40 million payroll, supplier industries, and secondary growth in the service sectors. The drumbeat of support for the transplant project shapes the agenda of public discussion by presenting one image of the community, and that is an image of economic growth. An alternative image of the community—as a place to live and work—is crowded off the public agenda. The transplant issue is debated on terms set by the political and business elites.

Persons from the social sector are hardly heard from in local and state newspapers. These are the persons and organizations who will have to deal with the impact of growth on the environment, schools, housing markets, transient populations, and other aspects of community life, and they have not been sought out by newspapers to provide their views on economic growth, auto transplants, or the incentive package. It is important to note that when labor did achieve some voice, as in the Kentucky newspapers, it was due primarily to its actions to oppose the transplants' antiunion policy. For example, organized labor in Kentucky was involved in a dispute over hiring practices by the Ohbayashi construction firm, which was building the Toyota plant. As a result of this dispute, labor organizations initiated several legal actions involving constitutional and environmental issues, which served to slow progress at the construction site until concessions were made to labor by the construction firm.

A similar situation took place in Tennessee, where organized labor was opposed to the nonunion hiring practices of the company hired to construct the Nissan plant. As a result, there were organized protests by labor at the Nissan ground-breaking ceremony, which resulted in several days of newspaper coverage of their concerns about nonunion hiring practices.

In both the Kentucky and Tennessee cases, what little space was provided to labor representatives in newspapers was the result of labor's protests, which were publicly visible and newsworthy, and not because newspapers sought out the views of labor as having legitimate questions about the transplant project.

The views of the education sector appeared in newspapers not in a questioning or critical voice, but in one describing possible relations between the university and the transplant, or discussions about special Saturday school arrangements that the state had promised to provide for children from Japanese families. The closest that the education sector came to raising questions about the transplants had to do with the impact on school population and the need for new schools (and hence higher taxes). This concern never developed to the level of a public issue, as city and county officials provided very low estimates of the number of additional children that would come into the district from Japanese families or production workers.

Thus, we may conclude from the data provided in Table 4.1 that a very narrow segment of the community had its views of the transplant project represented in the six newspapers that were analyzed. Clearly, the image of the community's influence structure was closer to the elitist than the populist end of the scale.

COSTS AND BENEFITS OF GROWTH

All articles were analyzed and coded for their discussion of topics that could be viewed as part of the costs and benefits of the transplant project. Table 4.2 provides a summary of topics that are viewed as positive toward growth and therefore on the benefits side of the ledger. Of the nine topics identified in articles, the one most frequently mentioned is new jobs, followed by other topics like the total payroll of new workers, and the general economic boost that the transplant will bring.

In each newspaper there was a heavy emphasis on jobs in front page stories ("Toyota Provides 3000 Jobs," "More Jobs for State Expected," and "There's Still Time to Apply at Auto Plant"), as well as spin-off industries ("Car Parts Firms Wheel Into State" and "Japanese Suppliers Interested in State"), and local economic growth ("New Shopping Plaza Planned," "Factory Sows Seeds of Growth," and "Nissan Decision Opens New Era for County"). These news stories about new jobs, new companies, and tax revenues were accompanied by "soft" news that was progrowth. These included human interest stories about Japanese families moving to the area ("New Life in Kentucky Not Without Its Problems" and "Japanese Family Enjoys New Life In Greater Lafayette"), "people on the street" stories, which contained interviews with and photos of eight community residents under the headline "Auto Plant Gets Community Support."

News stories frequently mention several topics, and we can see in the totals section of Table 4.2 that the number of topics mentioned often exceeds the number of articles written on transplants in the thirteen-month period under consideration. For example, newspapers in Kentucky on average mention several benefits topics in each article, i.e., 80 topics are presented in 60 articles for a 1.33 topics/articles ratio. This ratio

Table 4.2. Benefits of Growth Mentioned in Newspaper Articles

	Indiana newspapers				Kentucky newspapers				Tennessee newspapers			
	Local		State		Local		State		Local		State	
Topic	N	%	N	%	N	%	N	%	N	%	N	%
Boost economy	17	11.8	10	28.6	14	17.5	26	11.9	9	13.0	8	12.1
New jobs	65	45.1	16	45.7	26	32.5	64	29.4	32	46.4	21	31.8
Aggregate payroll	13	9.0	1	2.8	5	6.2	22	10.1	10	14.5	15	22.7
Spin-off growth	18	12.5	4	11.4	14	7.5	32	14.7	7	10.1	10	15.2
Higher land values	2	1.4	0	—	2	2.5	4	1.8	0	—	1	1.5
Higher standard of living	2	1.4	0	—	2	2.5	6	2.8	0	—	1	1.5
Salaries of new workers	10	6.9	3	8.6	3	3.8	5	2.3	4	5.8	3	4.5
Tax revenue	9	6.2	1	2.8	5	6.2	17	7.8	7	10.1	7	10.6
Experience of other workers	8	5.5	0	—	9	11.2	42	19.3	0	—	0	—
Total topics	144	99.8	35	99.9	80	99.9	218	100.1	69	99.9	66	99.9
Total articles	236		32		60		139		115		43	
Topics/articles	0.61		1.09		1.33		1.57		0.60		1.53	

provides a measure of the frequency with which the topics appear in newspapers.

If we turn to Table 4.3 we see a summary of the topics that are viewed as costs of growth, and therefore negative toward growth. In contrast to the benefits of growth (Table 4.2), which showed some uniformity across states, the costs of growth differ in each state. In Indiana, where only the local newspaper mentions costs, the negative topics are concentrated on land use issues ("Panel OKs Auto Plant Zoning Request" and "Recommendation: New Homes Go East of Auto Site") and displaced or disgruntled home owners ("Mobile Home Park Fate in Limbo," "Path to Auto Plant Cuts Across Yards," and "Residents Fight Park Evictions"). These topics raise the specter of state power used to acquire citizens' private property, and to change land use patterns. Both types of action use state power to harm some citizens in order to benefit others. The next largest category of topics involved tensions between Japanese and Americans because of the auto plant ("Auto Plant Dredges Up Ill Will" and "Fear of Racism Opens Rift Among Protesters").

In contrast to Indiana, the local newspaper in Kentucky identifies the costs of growth in the areas of pollution, incentives, and intergroup tensions. The state newspaper adds home owners' concerns and land use problems to the list. Immediately after the state of Kentucky made public its economic incentive package ("Governor Collins Unveils $125 million Incentive Package for Toyota"), constitutional lawyers raised questions about its legality ("State's Plan to Give Toyota Land May Be Unconstitutional") and labor leaders moved to a court test ("Two To Join Suit Over Toyota Plant Financing"). Local citizens, concerned about environmental problems, held public meetings ("Toyota Jobs Vs. Environmental Impact Debates," and "Scott County Families Seek Aid To Ensure Clean Water") and soon afterwards union officials challenged the state's issuance of a permit for air pollution control facilities at the Toyota plant ("2 Protest Toyota Pollution Permit"). Although these legal challenges slowed legislative action on the incentive package and construction at the plant site ("Toyota Plant Euphoria Sagging Under Load of Legal Documents"), the courts eventually ruled in favor of the state and Toyota on all matters.

In Tennessee, negative topics in local newspaper coverage are focused on incentives ("Farm Bureau on Record Against Nissan"), schools ("No Repay to Metro for Japanese Studies"), and intergroup tensions ("Nissan Road Routes Anger Neighborhood").

The totals section of Table 4.3 indicates that there are fewer costs of growth topics for each newspaper than the benefits of growth topics mentioned in Table 4.2. The ratio of cost topics to articles is smaller for Table 4.3 than for Table 4.2 for every newspaper. This indicates that

Table 4.3. Costs of Growth Mentioned in Newspaper Articles

| | Indiana newspapers | | | | Kentucky newspapers | | | | Tennessee newspapers | | | |
| | Local | | State | | Local | | State | | Local | | State | |
Topic	N	%	N	%	N	%	N	%	N	%	N	%
Land use, zoning	34	30.6	0	—	3	5.8	23	11.6	4	11.1	0	—
Displaced home owners	30	27.0	0	—	2	3.8	46	23.1	2	5.5	0	—
Pollution	9	8.1	0	—	14	26.9	53	26.6	2	5.5	1	10.0
Traffic congestion	8	7.2	1	20.0	2	3.8	10	5.0	4	11.1	1	10.0
Impact on schools	7	6.3	1	20.0	3	5.8	6	3.0	7	19.4	3	30.0
Intergroup tensions	20	18.0	3	60.0	8	15.3	17	8.5	6	16.7	0	—
Incentives; amount, legality	2	1.8	0	—	13	25.0	20	10.0	11	30.6	5	50.0
General changes in community	1	0.9	0	—	7	13.5	24	12.1	0	—	0	—
Total topics	111		5		52	99.9	199	99.9	36	99.9	10	100.0
Total articles	236		32		60		139		115		43	
Topics/articles	0.47		0.16		0.87		1.43		0.31		0.23	

positive topics about the transplants (benefits) are mentioned more frequently than are negative topics (costs).

It is also worth noting that state newspapers in Indiana and Tennessee are virtually silent on the costs of growth in contrast to their coverage of the benefits of growth. Only Kentucky's *Louisville Courier-Journal* provides roughly the same amount of coverage of both sides of the cost-benefits equation.

An alternative way of informing the public about costs and incentives would be to invite analysis by neutral third parties who could provide their expertise in examining projected costs and returns from the incentives. Instead, what is often presented are the state's figures without critical reaction. For example, Figure 4.1 appeared as a boxed item on the front page of the *Louisville Courier-Journal* (December 18, 1985).

These figures are presented without comment by anyone other than state officials. The balance sheet is quite clear, leading to the conclusion that the incentive package was "a wise initial investment." Unfortunately, the balance sheet is very unstable. On September 21, 1986, the *Lexington Herald Leader* reported that Toyota would be paying $5.6 million less in state taxes each year, which means that it would take longer for the state to recover its expenses. On October 14, 1986 the paper reported that recent estimates of site preparation put the cost at $43.9 million, which is $14.9 million above its earlier estimate. As if to counter the above overestimates of income and underestimates of costs, the *Louisville Courier-Journal* on October 24, 1986, ran the following headlined story: "Report Suggests Toyota Deal Could Pay Off for State within 20 Years." The story, however, is a little more equivocal than the headline:

> A state economist said yesterday that the $125 million incentive package pledged to Toyota Motor Corp. should pay off for the state in 20 years.
> But he also acknowledged that his analysis is incomplete, and that Kentucky might realize only a marginal gain or even a loss. (p. B1)

Further modification of revenue estimates would be reported on January 23, 1987, in the *Louisville Courier-Journal*. Apparently some of the $92 million in bonds issued by the state for the Toyota package have to be taxable bonds, rather than tax-exempt as assumed in original estimates. Some or all of the $60 million in bonds will be taxed at a 2 percent higher interest rate because they are not tax exempt. No estimate of the increased cost is provided in the story.

It is difficult to avoid the conclusion that newspapers do not wish to undertake a serious, impartial assessment of the costs and benefits of the incentive package. They probably believe they are providing a balanced assessment with a series of discrete stories, pointing out the pros and cons

Figure 4.1

TOYOTA'S COST—AND RETURN—TO STATE (over 20 years)

Kentucky's costs

Land purchase	$10,000,000
Site preparation	25,000,000
Training center	10,000,000
Employee training	33,000,000
Highway improvements	47,000,000
Total	$125,000,000

Other assistance:
Saturday school for Japanese children to be provided by University of Kentucky.
English classes for adults, children to be provided by Department of Education in cooperation with UK.

Kentucky tax recepts

Construction phase (3-year period)	
Construction firms	$2,174,300
Construction workers	3,283,600
Plant operation	
Toyota plant	$316,324,800
3000 plant workers	124,554,000
Weight-distance tax	920,400
1,900 non-manufacturing jobs*	41,634,000
Total	$488,891,100

*Based on U.S. Chamber of Commerce estimates.

of the state's financial incentives. But these stories are very inconclusive, and the state's estimates of costs and revenues are rarely subjected to any serious scrutiny.

The final part of our analysis of newspapers and the transplants involves the amount of coverage in column inches of newspaper space for stories about the transplants. The space provided for articles is classified as active-positive ("Hopes Ride High On Auto Plant"), negative ("Homeless: Auto Plant Causes Concern"), passive-positive ("Kentucky's Man In Japan Knows Value of Patience"), or mixed ("Progress Takes Bite Out of Couple's Front Yard"). The active-positive and negative articles are either overwhelmingly pro- or antitransplant in tone and content. The passive-positive articles are seemingly neutral articles because they objectively describe progress at the plant site, provide details of the employee recruitment plan, or descriptions of the state's incentive package without endorsing, criticizing, or questioning the accounts. They are considered to be passive-positive because they tacitly endorse or accept the states' and automakers' actions.

Table 4.4 indicates that positive articles on the transplants were given substantially more space than negative articles in five of the six newspapers. If the passive-positive articles are added to the active-positive articles, the positive coverage was seven times greater in Indiana, and two to three times greater in Tennessee. In Kentucky, the local newspaper gave greater coverage to negative stories than to the positive stories.

The *Lexington Herald-Leader*, the local newspaper in Kentucky, is the exception to the general pattern of positive coverage exceeding negative coverage. The dominance of negative coverage stems from the very active opposition to Toyota and the state's incentive package that came from labor, environmentalists, and the small-business community. Apparently the local newspaper felt that it could not avoid giving coverage to the forces of opposition, but the state newspaper had less trouble ignoring the negative coverage. The legal actions by local labor, environmentalists, and small-business owners could not be ignored by the hometown newspaper as readily as it could by the state newspaper. This may be due to a combination of economic and moral pressure applied to the newspaper by its "neighbors." The more geographically remote Louisville newspaper could more easily turn a deaf ear to those who oppose growth or the transplant.

HOW NEWSPAPERS DEAL WITH DISSIDENT VOICES

The preceding analysis of how newspapers cover the transplant projects in their states indicates that only selected segments of the commu-

Table 4.4. Amount of Newspaper Space Devoted to Positive/Negative Stories about Transplants

Theme	Indiana newspapers				Kentucky newspapers				Tennessee newspapers			
	Local		State		Local		State		Local		State	
	Sq. in.	%	Sq. in.	%	Sq. in.	%	Sq. in.	%	Sq. in.	%	Sq. in.	%
Active-positive: new jobs, spin-off industries, economic growth	1,709	31.0	1,166	70.3	1,251	21.9	2,810	32.3	2,660	52.0	1,425	55.5
Negative: criticism of incentives, lawsuits, intergroup tensions	465	8.4	183	11.0	2,539	44.4	1,680	19.3	1,129	22.1	676	26.3
Passive-positive building site progress, employee selection plans, description of incentive package	1,512	27.4	222	13.4	756	13.2	1,847	21.2	775	15.1	56	2.2
Mixed land use plan, assessments, easements, evictions, environmental impact	1,832	33.2	88	5.3	1,174	20.5	2,357	27.1	553	10.8	411	16.0
Total space	5,520	100.0	1,659	100.0	5,720	100.0	8,694	99.9	5,117	100.0	2,568	100.0
Total artices	236		32		60		139		115		43	
Space/articles	23.4		51.8		95.3		62.5		44.5		59.7	

nity are allowed to speak on the topic, and that coverage of the transplant project is overwhelmingly positive in terms of space, topic, and tone. Yet despite this blanket of progrowth coverage, the voices of those opposed to the project or those who have a different concept of community do manage to break through the newspapers' filtering frame of the grow-or-die community.

The most direct approach to dealing with dissident voices is simply to ignore them when reporting stories about the transplants. It was reported that letters critical of Honda or the Japanese were not printed in central Ohio newspapers (Gelsanliter 1990:172). It was also reported that six television stations in Louisville and Lexington rejected union-sponsored advertisements that were critical of hiring practices at the construction site of the Toyota plant (*Louisville Courier-Journal*, August 6, 1986, p. E8).

The more typical approach is to present negative or critical information within the context of balanced information. The practice is what Gaye Tuchman (1972) calls an "objectivity ritual" of professional journalism. For example, Indiana's local newspaper presented a 43-square-inch story about an out-of-state town with a new Japanese auto plant that is experiencing severe traffic problems and overcrowding in its schools. The article points to the failure of the state government to follow through on the commitment it made when the incentive package was developed. Lafayette residents reading such an article might understandably raise questions about whether the Subaru-Isuzu plant might also bring more problems than people expected. In the same issue of the newspaper, however, there is a shorter article (twenty square inches) about why there should be fewer traffic problems or school enrollments as a result of the Lafayette auto plant. There is also a forty-four-square-inch article about how to apply for one of the 1,700 new jobs at the plant where the "average worker will earn $30,000 a year." Thus, the newspaper's article that was potentially critical of the new industrial venture was easily defused by the simultaneous publication of two additional items stressing the positive aspects of the new plant.

The Louisville state newspaper provides another example of how to marginalize dissenting voices. A lengthy news story (ninety-eight square inches) under the headline "Official Hopes Auto Plant Spurns His County" is about a county official who is opposed to the state's effort to attract Toyota. The official is quoted as saying, "If they say we want this in Kentucky just to say 'We're bigger, we've got more industry here and we've got more jobs here, but it's not doing you any good—how can you call it progress?" This quote is followed by the statement, "His is the lone voice of dissent among county and city leaders hoping to have the big Japanese car and truck assembly plant." Moreover, the dissident official's views are covered in thirteen square inches, with the remaining eighty-five square inches devoted to the views of eight state and local officials, business leaders, and economists, which are different from or critical of the dissident.

It is probably relatively easy for newspapers to deal with criticism when it is aimed at specific aspects of the incentive package, or the long-term benefits to the community of the transplant project. The pro- and anti-incentive views can be presented within the framework of the "objectivity ritual" discussed earlier. Readers are left with the feeling that there is an honest difference of opinion on whether or not the state will benefit from the transplant. These are not emotional issues, but practical questions that call for rational, dispassionate examination of the facts by experts.

However, sometimes the voices of dissent seem to reach a gut level, a feeling of discomfort or opposition that does not lend itself to cost-benefit analyses. Since the dissident voices are expressed on a symbolic or emotional level, it is difficult for the newspapers to counter the criticisms without attacking the critics. We examine an example of this type of dissent in the Ota City Drive controversy in Lafayette, Indiana, home of Subaru-Isuzu.

In May 1989 the mayor of Lafayette visited Ota, Japan, home of Fuji Heavy Industries, along with seventeen other Lafayette residents. On returning home, the mayor announced the formation of a committee to work on cultural exchanges between Ota and Lafayette, to strengthen their sister city ties.

In March 1990, four months after the opening of the Subaru-Isuzu plant, the mayor proposed to the city council that a street in the city's main public park be changed from Cherokee Drive to Ota City Drive. The street is located next to a spot in the park called Memorial Island, which contains a plaque honoring the county's dead servicemen.

In mid-April three letters to the editor are published that are critical of the mayor's proposal. They all suggest other locations for the proposed street name and ask for respect for the feelings of veterans. Immediately following the letters the paper prints an editorial entitled "A Fresh Perspective on Japan," in which it discusses "Japan-bashing" and criticizes those in the United States "who are trying to make Japan the scapegoat for their economic sins and political blunders" (*Lafayette Journal and Courier*, April 18, 1990). It is worth noting that none of the proveterans' letters mentioned trade balances or the Subaru-Isuzu plant, which the editorial uses to account for Japan-bashing.

A front-page story on May 8, 1990, announces "Council OKs Ota City Drive." The story tells of the city council meeting attended by more than fifty veterans who opposed the council's decision. The council members are reported to have "called on veterans to accept the hand of friendship and peace." The very next paragraph states: "After the vote, a bitter group of veterans from World War II and the Korean and Vietnam Wars slowly filed out of the council chambers, slinging a few racial slurs, condemning council members as ungrateful and threatening to destroy the Ota City Drive sign when it's installed." The remainder of the story quotes the mayor's call for compromise and friendship and his statement that the renaming is not meant to desecrate the memory of those who died in World War II, and a series of angry and hostile comments by veterans. It is not until the end of the story that it is reported that two council members voted against the proposed name change.

Five days later on May 13, another front -page story states: "Ota Drive Opens Old Wounds for Vets." The story opens: "A veteran group's angry reaction to the renaming of a park street as Ota City Drive does not represent the feelings of most Greater Lafayette residents, some community leaders say." This lengthy story serves primarily to reorganize the views of the veterans by contrasting their "hostile" views with those of "reasonable" people.

An editorial on "Memorial Day: 3 Viewpoints" appeared on May 28. It calls for "extending hands of friendship and partnership to Japan, a World War II enemy, by naming a public street for a 'sister city,' Ota, Japan." The editorial appears to be anticipating the planned Memorial Day ceremonies in the local park, at the site of the proposed Ota City Drive next to Memorial Island. The May 29 paper contains a dramatic front-page photo of six men, World War II veterans wearing VFW caps, standing up facing the camera lens. In the background is the mayor standing before a speaker's platform surrounded by American flags. The veterans have turned their backs to the stage during the mayor's speech. The headline is: "Despite Protests, Vets Remembered," and the two opening paragraphs are as follows:

> When a group of about 35 veterans turned their backs on Mayor James F. Riehle during memorial Day services in Columbian Park, Bill Shelby was embarrassed, ashamed, and sick to his stomach.
> Shelby, himself a veteran, chastised those veterans who wanted to turn Monday into a day of contempt instead of a day of remembrance.

The remainder of the story describes events of the parade, the number of veterans' groups that marched to the park, but broke ranks before entering the park, and the comments of bystanders. An editorial the following day (May 30) is very critical of the veterans, stating that "some of what they have said and done smacks of racism."

On July 13 the newspaper featured a story "Ota Drive Stance Changes," which discusses the mayor's plan to ask the city council to reverse the name change at a special meeting on July 23. He called upon city residents and civic organizations for suggestions of alternative streets that could be given the name of Lafayette's sister city. As part of the story, the newspaper has a special boxed form labeled "What to Name Ota" and calls on readers to use the form to send suggestions to the newspaper. The form states that the paper will publish the list of suggested ideas.

On July 15 the paper editorialized "Get New Ota City Drive Ready," calling upon the city council to select a new location for the street before the old one is dropped. The editorial mentions two possible locations, which were what was suggested by veterans groups months ago at the start of the controversy.

On July 16, a final editorial on the subject states: "Larger Issues Than Ota Drive," and suggests that the Ota City Drive issue pales by comparison with the other major issues facing "modern-day Lafayette." The editorial calls for public input and government action in dealing with street repair, sewage treatment, environmental clean-up, police/fire protection, and affordable housing. These are certainly issues that affect a broad segment of the community, and about which there is likely to be greater unanimity than was found in the Ota City Drive controversy.

The point of this issue is that political officials and the newspaper devoted considerable resources to trying to overcome opposition to an action by the mayor and city council that had great symbolic significance for veterans' groups and other residents. The newspaper chose to associate some of the opponents with racism and Japan-bashing. Political leaders and newspaper editors refused to give legitimacy to the concerns of veterans' groups because they didn't want their community to be tainted with a redneck image. Interviews with representatives of veterans' groups conducted by the author revealed the kind of patriotism often associated with working-class veterans—a genuine reverence for certain symbols that they believe have great meaning, and that can be damaged or destroyed by association with the proposed name change. Perhaps an old-fashioned kind of patriotism, even naive in the 1990s, but hardly racism. The veterans also seemed genuine in their suggestions of alternative sites for Ota City Drive, which if acted upon by city officials would have avoided the entire controversy.

The effort to discredit veterans' groups who publicly opposed actions to further the corporatist project in Indiana is similar to the media coverage of public protests by organized labor in Kentucky and Tennessee. The Indiana protest was a symbolic issue, but in the other two states the issue involved the role of union workers during the construction phase of the transplants. Each of these protests included persons who probably made racist comments, and whose views are certainly objectionable. But the protests were not necessarily racist in their origin.

Supporters of the corporatist project from the political and business community and from the news media seem to feel that the corporatist project is fragile and cannot tolerate voices of opposition that are given legitimacy. The ideology of corporatism is so driven by the image of a new partnership where everyone wins that supporters of the ideology seem unable to understand why everyone does not see it the same way.

When all of this newspaper coverage is considered from the perspective of corporatism, we have an image of a new cooperative spirit between government, business, and sometimes labor. Even when there are disputes, as in the case of Toyota and labor in Kentucky, the resolution is portrayed within a cooperative framework in the local newspapers: "Unions and Toyota Resolve Hiring Dispute," "Toyota Builder, Unions Reach Agreement." A joint statement released by the AFL-CIO and Ohbayashi (builders of the plant for Toyota) states that the agreement was "to enhance the employment opportunities and other benefits for the people of Kentucky by assuring the success of this project and those which follow its lead, throughout the United States" (*Lexington Herald-Leader*, November, 1986, p. 1; *Louisville Courier-Journal*, November 26, 1986, p. 1).

CONCLUSIONS

This analysis of how six newspapers covered the transplant projects in three states indicates that, with the possible exception of a less enthusiastic *Lexington Herald-Leader*, newspapers provided very positive support for the transplants. The accounts of the new automobile plants in the newspapers stressed the views of public officials and business leaders, and provided much less coverage of persons from other community sectors. Moreover, the content and coverage of news items stressed the positive aspects of both general economic growth and the specific state-supported efforts to attract Japanese auto plants.

There seems to be little reason to doubt that newspapers functioned as cheerleaders for their community's growth machine. Their actions are consistent with a view of newspapers as part of a growth coalition with profit-oriented interests similar to those of political and business elites. When they create stories about a new industry and about its potential contribution to the community, they make choices about the image of community they wish to project, the points of view to be represented, and what constitutes a balance of views. It seems clear that the newspaper coverage examined in this chapter did not present readers with a sufficiently broad range of questions and information about the costs and benefits of the new plant, and about the wisdom of using public money to acquire and develop land for private corporations and to fund their recruitment and training programs. As a consequence, newspapers appear to be less interested in educating their communities about the costs and benefits of growth than they are in promoting growth.

Chapter 5

Creating a New Worker: Fusing Labor, Community, and Company

We try to include the family in the business. You win the whole family over.
The whole family loves the company and wants to do the best for it. And the
employee gets that support at home.
                    —Nissan executive, *Nashville Tennessean*, July 17, 1983

A community will most truly prosper culturally and economically through a
collective effort. . . .It is our goal to help preserve and improve the quality
of life here in the Bluegrass.
                    —Toyota vice president, *Lexington Herald-Leader*, October 5, 1988

We are not merely seeking employees, but associates with whom we can
build a lasting relationship.
                    —SIA executive, *Lafayette Journal and Courier*, September 12, 1987

After selecting sites for each of the six transplants, the next two to three
years were devoted to the construction phase of the project. Construction
was carried out by numerous contractors and subcontractors who would
be responsible for getting a vast production system ready for a specified
start date. During this time, Japanese management would turn its attention to building the technical, interorganizational, and human components of a production system of proven success in Japan. In this chapter
we examine how the transplants would develop the kind of work force
needed for the Japanese system of production. The process of developing
this work force would take place in four distinct phases: (1) prerecruitment community socialization, (2) recruitment socialization, (3) work
group training, and (4) continuous in-plant culture.

105

PRERECRUITMENT COMMUNITY SOCIALIZATION

During the months devoted to the construction of the transplants, people in the host communities would learn about how the new corporations view workers, the social organization of work, and worker-management relations. Representatives of the transplants, using mainly local newspaper stories, but sometimes talks at the local university or the Chamber of Commerce, informed potential employees and the friends and relatives of potential employees about what it would be like to work in a transplant. A typical approach would be to contrast the "old worker" and the "new worker" using examples from another transplant. For example, the NUMMI plant in California was a Toyota-GM joint venture, and the first Japanese auto transplant in the United States. Here is what Kentuckians learned about NUMMI from stories in the *Lexington Herald-Leader* (April 23, 1986).

In the late 1970s when the auto plant was a GM facility there were 6,500 workers and over 5,000 shop-floor grievances. Labor-management relations were adversarial, with very little basis for cooperation. After the NUMMI joint venture was started there were 2,550 employees (85 percent from the former plant) *but only 20 grievances on file*. The president of the United Auto Workers Local 2244 attributes the change to the new management system:

> When you get people involved and when you give people the right to have a say-so at the work site, a right to share their ideas, when you solicit their ideas and experience and make them feel an integral part of that, then the end result is a quality product and a more harmonious worker.

Other newspaper stories about the transplants would emphasize the new relationship of trust between workers and Japanese management. American workers learn about the sincerity of the Japanese and that you can trust their word. The value of this trust would often be discussed in connection with the implicit commitment not to lay off workers, even in tough economic times. Such matters are often juxtaposed with the numerous closings at unionized U.S. auto plants.

A Japanese middle-management employee at one of the transplants, who gives talks to local groups, describes some of what he says to Americans about Japanese business practices.

> Once we are hired by a large company after having graduated from a university, we keep working at the same company until retirement. Even though the situation is changing, the majority of people still stay with the same company. A person is not fired or laid off as long as he doesn't inflict a

major loss upon the company which he works for even if he has contributed no major achievements.

This lifetime employment system, which is called *Shushin Koyou* in Japanese, brings about intense loyalty to the company which a person belongs to. For example, the Subaru employee parking lot is full of Subaru cars. The other example is Isuzu employees. They don't drink Kirin beer, which belongs to the Mitsubishi group, because Kirin beer is transported by Mitsubishi trucks in Japan and not by Isuzu trucks.

Due to this loyalty, most Japanese companies have a good relationship between labor and management.

Other messages that were reaching the community and potential employees were concerned with the attitudes of American workers and the new work arrangements in the transplants. Although American workers are viewed as intelligent, they are also believed to be too individualistic and not able to see the value of teamwork. Under Japanese-style management, emphasis will be placed on small work teams whose members share information and share the work load at the assembly line. On the latter point, Kentuckians are told that transplant workers will learn to rotate among many different jobs rather than specializing in only one assignment on the line. This means that workers can help each other, substitute for each other, and rotate assignments according to the demands of the production schedule.

The important thing about these prerecruitment media stories is that they serve as a kind of *anticipatory* socialization of potential transplant employees before the actual recruitment begins. Workers who are dedicated to the idea of a union or opposed to the team concept or job rotation may choose not to apply for work in the transplant, or if they do, they may begin to reassess the importance of their earlier preferences.

A second important aspect of this early media coverage of the transplant is that it conveys a message of a shared fate among labor, community, and the transplant, in a project that is much larger than the narrow interests of any person or group. Newspaper stories remind the reader repeatedly of the company's $800 million investment; of the two thousand production workers to be hired; of the $40 million payroll that will flow into the county; of the spin-off companies and thousands of jobs that will follow the transplant. And even before any of these things come to pass, there will be two to three years of construction with over one thousand workers and an $11 million payroll.

The enormity of the state-transplant project as presented in local newspapers reduces concerns about traffic congestion or pollution, nonunion contractors, or schooling problems to the level of petty complaints. Concern about the project, or opposition to the project, is marginalized as short-sighted and idiosyncratic. Consider, for example, the following headline and opening line in a news story that is critical of the transplant project:

Several Residents Concerned for Land

Along with the excitement and expectation that has followed the recent announcement that the world's fourth largest auto maker, Nissan Motor Company, will construct a multimillion dollar truck assembly plant near Smyrna, there has been concern. (*Murfreesboro Daily News Journal*, December 1, 1980)

The complaint that follows cannot help but be disproportionately weak in the face of the transplant project. The message is clear: Nothing less than the future of the community is at stake, and nothing less than community, workers, and company working together can make the project a reality.

RECRUITMENT SOCIALIZATION

Long before any of the transplants would begin the process of hiring production workers local newspapers provided estimates of the number of persons expected to apply for the new jobs. The *Louisville Courier-Journal* (September 10, 1986) reported that the state expected 200,000 people to apply for 3,000 jobs at Toyota. The *Lafayette Journal and Courier* (June 14, 1987) estimated that 50,000 are expected to apply for 1,700 jobs at SIA. Mazda reported having a pool of 96,500 job applicants for 3,500 jobs (Fucini and Fucini 1990).

Regardless of the accuracy of these estimates of potential job applicants, their presentation to the public can have a number of consequences that are favorable for the transplants. First, the general public and potential applicants are given the clear impression that working for a transplant is very desirable, and that the new employer enjoys support across the community. In addition, anyone choosing to enter into the lengthy selection process must have a strong commitment, given that the chances of being hired are a long-shot of twenty-five or fifty to one. A third positive consequence is that the workers who are eventually hired will undoubtedly view themselves as special, an elite work force that is different from other autoworkers. On the reverse side, applicants who do not make it might not harbor resentment or negative feelings that they have been judged unfairly. When you are competing for a job against two or three other candidates you are more likely to entertain thoughts of favoritism or bias in the selection decision, but when your chances are fifty to one you may see the selection as based on objective grounds. One worker who successfully completed the selection process felt he was treated very fairly: "It gave guys like me, who didn't know the right people, a chance [and] the testing really tapped into my potential" (Graham 1991:63).

One of the more impressive examples of a transplant's effort to shape public consciousness was by Toyota, as it prepared for an open house to celebrate the opening of its plant in Georgetown, Kentucky. On October 4, 1988, a full-page ad in the *Lexington Herald-Leader* contained a half-page photo of a young man, in his midtwenties, in a button-down shirt with an open collar. Above the photo it said: "When I looked at the future I got scared." Below the photo was the following text:

> Maybe he would have moved away to some big city somewhere and gotten a chance that way. But he didn't want to move. "I was born and raised in Lexington, Kentucky," he says, "this is home. This is where I want to stay." He was bright, ambitious, and unlucky; he was in the right place at the wrong time. "I got a college degree in 1985," he says, "a B.A. in marketing, but there were no jobs. None that would give me a future anyway. There are some fine companies in Lexington, and big ones too. But no one was hiring."
>
> He checked the want ads everyday—for three years. He sent out hundreds of resumes. And meanwhile he took a job that wasn't quite right for him. "The people there were very nice," he says, "they were great. But the job wasn't taking me anywhere. After a couple of years I began to feel stalled, stuck. When I looked at the future I got scared."
>
> Then Toyota arrived; we started building a billion dollar auto plant just outside of Lexington.
>
> When we started hiring, he deluged us with five separate applications. That's how badly he wanted to work with us.
>
> When we finally met him, we were impressed with his drive. "My name's Rob Wehrle," he said, "and I'll take anything you've got. Just give me a chance. Let me show what I can do."
>
> And that's just what he's doing. And he's not the only one. His story is but one of more than a thousand stories at our new plant in Kentucky— which will be officially dedicated this week.
>
> Soon there will be thousands more.
>
> Toyota

The next day there was a twelve-page supplement on Toyota in the paper. One page looks at "Training—A Top Priority from Start to Finish." Photos and accompanying story stress quality of work, reduction of waste, and creating "multi-skilled employees rather than workers who only know a specific craft." Another page has the headline: "Japanese, American Workers Share Common Ground." Photos and story emphasize mutual respect, support, friendships. "Despite the differences [in culture] the Japanese and American workers have managed to find common ground"—Toyota. "We share the Toyota culture."

On the day of the open house, October 9, the newspaper joined in the celebration without the assistance of paid advertising. The front-page headline of the *Louisville Courier-Journal* reads: "Scott Countians Get First Peek at Toyota Plant." There are three large photos with quotes beneath each: The first is of a young child in front of a 1958 Toyopet, the first Toyota in the United States. The woman in the photo is whispering in her grandson's ear: "Maybe you'll work here someday." A second group photo carries the caption: "It makes us a spot on the map. You used to say you were from Georgetown, right down the road from Lexington. Now you're from Georgetown where the Toyota plant is." The third photo is of a couple in the plant, saying: "I was just awed, amazed. I couldn't imagine anything like that in my wildest dreams."

The photos and text from the advertisements and the news coverage obviously represent a very controlled and selective reality. Especially since the newspaper announcements inviting "Scott Countians" to the open house provided maps, showed parking areas, and added the notice: "No Cameras Please."

The media blitz that started on October 4 ended on October 11 with another full-page ad: a large photo of a door, with caption: "This door leads to a different world." The text below states:

> It's one of the doors to our new billion dollar automotive plant in George-town, Kentucky, just outside of Lexington. If you go through it you'll find yourself in a different world. The people in that world are mostly Americans. They're independent, creative, impatient for progress. And together we're making cars—800 cars a day when we get up to speed, providing jobs for 3,500 people, and indirectly creating employment for tens of thousands more. Our plant was officially dedicated on October 6. So now it's official: We're open for business in America. Our business is making the best of two worlds.
>
> Toyota

In addition to the transplant ads and newspaper accounts of the thousands of persons who would be applying for jobs, potential applicants were told that the selection process could be lengthy, involving a variety of mental, physical, and group tests. Hill et al. (1989) describe the selection process at Mazda as having five steps:

1. Two hours of written tests covering mechanical, oral, and numerical skills.
2. A personal interview about prior work experience and suitability for work at Mazda.

3. Simulated social situations designed to assess how an applicant deals with interpersonal problems.
4. Medical examination including tests for substance abuse.
5. Physical tasks permitting assessment of an applicant's ability to do the actual jobs at Mazda.

Hill reports that workers stated that the testing described above often extended over six months, with weeks elapsing before applicants were informed about whether or not they had passed a test.

Graham (1991) describes a very similar selection process at Subaru-Isuzu as she experienced it as a job applicant. She submitted an application on February 3, and on June 30, after months of screening, received a phone call to report for work on July 10. During the five-month selection period, Graham describes a process that is very much like what applicants faced at Mazda, as depicted by Hill above. There were paper and pencil General Aptitude Test Batteries; questionnaires assessing attitudes toward teamwork, group problem-solving, and interest in learning new skills; small-group problem-solving under time pressure, where each individual's actions were recorded by observers; simulated tasks that assessed physical dexterity and endurance, as well as individual and team problem-solving; physical examination, including drug testing; and interviews with an individual team leader and a pair of team leaders.

Interviews with an assessment coordinator at one of the transplants described a seven-phase process that started with fifty-four thousand completed applications and ended with approximately two thousand hired workers. Phase I involved advertising and recruitment. Interested parties usually obtained applications at the state Department of Employment. Phase II, Orientation and Application Process, had several steps and required at least two different appointments. The first step was completing a state application form and providing a ten-year work history. The completed application and work history forms were sent to the plant for screening by the Japanese. The assessment coordinator said, "I think the Japanese would screen out people who had extensive experience in the U.S. auto industry. They did not want to have to untrain people who had the U.S. autoworkers' bad habits." Applicants were then scheduled for another appointment to take a General Aptitude Test Battery and to view a video about what it means to be an associate at the transplant.

The assessment coordinator showed me the video and said it was designed to give applicants a realistic picture of expectations for associates and would lead some applicants to self-select out of the selection process. The video opens with indoor scenes of the plant and of associates in Japan and in the U.S. facility. A combination of audio and printed statements announces: "The future has arrived. We are seeking a team of associates who share our values. Together we must beat the competition."

The rest of the video outlines the values of the transplants through scenes of workers and printed messages.

[1] Team approach—Help out others
    Teams frequently meet on their own time
[2] Quality is the top priority
    All associates take part in quality discussion groups
[3] Kaizen means searching for a better way
[4] We must eliminate waste throughout the company
    Working weekends or overtime when needed
    Work tempo is fast and consistent
[5] Work flexibility—Multi-talented workers
    Be prepared for changes at any time
[6] Job security is important to all of us
    Continuous training leads to security
    Security means safety
[7] Our spirit is enthusiastic involvement
    Come to work everyday on time
[8] Open communication builds mutual trust

Phase III, Initial Screening and Assessment, was conducted at the plant in a special space set aside for worker selection. This phase had two separate steps, requiring different appointments. The first appointment involved completion of another application form for the company (different from the application form completed for the state in Phase II), completion of a Job Fit Inventory questionnaire, and several small-group problem-solving tasks. Those who successfully completed this step were invited for Phase IV, which was a second full-day session involving two work simulations. One simulation was called the "fuel assembly," and it involved hoses, clamps, filters, gauges, and tools. There was a specific way to assemble the parts and the task was timed. The second simulation was the "wheel assembly" involving tire rims, wheel nuts, and tools. According to the assessment coordinator,

When we did our work simulations we wanted to see if they could handle time pressure, physical demands, and had any ideas about how to do it differently. After each simulation we asked for suggestions about how to organize the task differently. Some suggested locating tools or parts in different locations. Some suggested color-coded hoses or filters. We were looking for people with new ideas. If someone said, "The way you showed them to do it was fine"—they were out!

Phase V was devoted to a check on the applicant's references and in-plant interviews with only a subset of the applicants who were being considered for special positions. Phase VI required another appointment for a health assessment by those applicants who received favorable reviews by assessors. A general physical examination and a drug and alcohol screening took place at a local health facility. Most applicants who reached the health assessment phase were scheduled for in-plant interviews the same day. One to three weeks following this phase, letters or phone calls were made to tell people when to report for work. Phase VII, On-the-Job-Observation, once people had started working, was designed to give assessors and team leaders a chance to see if the new hires were well suited for their assignments.

It is important to note that the recruitment and training procedures discussed by the assessment coordination are not the creation of a training group hired by the state and/or the transplant. Rather, they were described and specified in great detail in the Memorandum of Understanding containing the state's commitments to the transplant. The pre-employment screening and employment training process to be undertaken by the state begins with the following statement about Indiana's training package:

1. Establish Partnership of Fuji-Isuzu and Indiana's Employment & Training professionals through Visit to Japan. Upon the selection and announcement of a plant site in Indiana, immediate arrangements (within 60 days) will be made for a team of Indiana Employment and Training officials to visit Fuji-Isuzu training officials in Japan. The objectives of this trip will be to:

A. Develop a detailed understanding of the work force requirements and qualifications needed by Fuji-Isuzu. This is an essential requirement in order to recruit and train the joint venture work force.

B. Begin building a team relationship with Fuji-Isuzu in order to ensure a timely plant launch.

C. Begin to develop a comprehensive plan for the employment and training portion of the Joint Venture project.

The point of this is to indicate that recruitment screening and selection and employment training were under the control of the transplant, thereby ensuring that they, and not an Indiana group of trainers, would set forth the procedures and criteria to be followed for screening, selecting, and training the work force.

At the end of the interview, the assessor was asked to reexamine the selection system he used, and to consider criticism that the process was an example of overkill:

A.   No U.S. firm, large or small, has ever done anything like this. But remember, they got a lot of state funds to do it. I don't know if they would have invested that much of their own money in the process.

Q.   Some say that the Japanese do the same thing in their plants in Japan.

A.   I don't know about that. I went to Japan to learn their way of doing things. It's a different tradition there in hiring. Many children still think about following their fathers in the same plant. When you have this kind of tradition you don't have to think about a worker's commitment.

Q.   Why did you use so many steps in the selection process, requiring applicants to make a number of appointments?

A.   The selection process could have been collapsed. We purposely had more steps than we needed. Only the most committed people would go through all those assessments over several months.

Q.   Did you ever select for location? Trying to get people from the county or state?

A.   We never used location. It turned out that about half were from the state.

Q.   Did you ever select for race or gender?

A.   We enhanced the GATB scores [General Aptitude Test Battery] of minorities to get them into the pool. But it didn't do much good. Eventually you were going to compete with people with better scores. When you are eventually comparing task performances of applicants who have true 98th percentile scores with applicants who have enhanced percentile scores the first group will win out.

Q.   What about women?

A.   We never tried to get a certain number of women as far as I know.

Q.   Some say that your selection process was also aimed at screening out prounion types.

A.   That's an interesting issue. You know, the Japanese changed their priorities during the assessment process. At the beginning we put considerable stress on initiative as one of the qualities we were looking for in applicants. But after we got into the screening and assessment process they started to say forget about initiative. Let's get people who will follow orders. Forget about people who are always questioning, who show too much leadership. They got very sensitive about applicants who showed too much initiative. I thought the union would really try to get in here. But not much so far. There have been some efforts to contact workers or to get their people in the plant, but as long as they are paying sixteen dollars an hour and no layoffs, forget about a union.

Q.   What are you doing about new hires?

A.   There are no new hires. They use temporary people for any replacements. Besides they have had only 1 percent turnover in their original pool. That's phenomenal.

Q.   So how do you feel about the entire selection process?

A.   I think the whole process has been very valid. The best evidence is that we haven't had a single challenge by someone who didn't get a job. We have extensive documentation at every stage. We have behavioral data from multiple assessors. It's not just based on opinions anymore. Many U.S. firms are starting to follow this process because it works.

Comparable detailed information on the selection process at all transplants is not available. Gelsanliter reports that Nissan required applicants to "take 40 to 200 hours of unpaid preemployment training, which they could do at night or on weekends so they wouldn't have to take time off from other jobs" (1992:66). Toyota's practice of requiring fourteen hours of written tests covering aptitude and dexterity met with some criticism in Kentucky newspapers because it would discourage many local job applicants without a high school diploma (p. 187).

Hill et al. (1989) describe the selection process as part of an effort to match a work force with a corporate culture. Graham (1991) views it as part of a new way to exercise control over workers. Both interpretations focus on the activities of workers within the plant, and they make good sense. However, there are two additional aspects to the selection process that relate to our general view of the new worker, who symbolizes the coming together of community, labor, and company. First, Graham (1991:64) describes the two or three thousand workers who successfully completed the selection process as sharing a feeling of genuine accomplishment in having come through a long and demanding process. They almost seem analogous to the young Marine recruits who survive the rigors of boot camp, emerging with an extraordinary sense of pride and invincibility (albeit unrealistic, to say the least). When these two or three thousand new workers are viewed in the context of their personal networks in relatively small communities, we can anticipate how rapidly good feelings about the transplant can spread.

The second aspect of the new worker as a symbolic blend of community, labor, and company is reflected in those who act as selectors or socializers of the recruits. While we lack complete information, we know that in the cases of Toyota, Nissan, and SIA, the earliest stages of recruitment were handled by the states' Department of Employment. Moreover, some aspect of the selection process (or training process after selection) was paid for with state funds, whether it be the $5 per hour that Kentucky paid for time spent in assessment, the $10.20 an hour paid by Kentucky for up to six months of in-plant training, or Indiana's payment of transportation, lodging, and meals for the hundreds of team leaders who are trained in Japan. This is a case of Hoosier job applicants, being selected by Hoosier testers and evaluators, paid for by Hoosier taxpayers.

Thus, the selection of employees by the transplants is more than simply finding workers with the best intellectual, physical, and attitudinal qualifications to work in teams with high productivity and commitment to quality. It is also a way of selling *corporatism* as the new partnership between capital and community where everyone wins.

WORK GROUP TRAINING

After being hired, successful recruits enter a period of additional training ranging from three weeks to three months. Hill et al. (1989) describe a three-week "soft" orientation at Mazda when associates meet Mazda executives and are exposed to the *kaizen* philosophy of continuous improvement. This is followed by two additional periods in the factory, where recruits are assigned to a shop to watch, listen, and get some hands-on experience.

Graham (1991) also went through a three-week "orientation and training" phase at SIA after the training was completed. Her experiences were similar to those reported by Mazda recruits in their three weeks of soft orientation. About 40 percent of the time was devoted to discussing company policies on wages and benefits, and to classes on work rules, car engineering, use of basic tools, blueprint reading, safety, and maintenance. The other 60 percent of the three-week period was devoted to discussion of the company's philosophy of quality production, *kaizen* lessons, and sensitivity to interpersonal and cross-cultural interaction. Most of these topics seem to lay the foundation for the work team, which is the basic unit of production in the assembly plants.

The work team is typically composed of eight to a dozen members, the number varying across different workstations. Team members are cross-trained and therefore able to assist each other and to take over the jobs of those who are sick or on vacation. Cross-training is facilitated by the Japanese approach of having very few job classifications. In contrast, U.S. auto plants have hundreds of job classifications and workers are involved in only one activity, in which they specialize. Fucini and Fucini (1990) report that when Mazda executives negotiated with the United Auto Workers who would be representing Mazda workers, they insisted on having only two job categories (production and skilled trades) and that "Mazda managers would have the freedom to transfer workers from job to job, to redesign jobs as they saw fit, and to assign overtime work when necessary without being impeded by restrictive work rules" (p. 16).

It is expected that work teams will develop strong interpersonal bonds of respect and friendship, in the hope that they will facilitate the communication and cooperation that is essential for a productive team.

IN-PLANT CULTURE

The transplants are involved in the conscious construction of an in-plant culture that will reinforce the principles of organization and inter-personal relationship that guided the selection and training of new employees. These principles include worker participation; trust between workers and management; common goals of the community, workers, and the company; and the company's commitment to put people first by guaranteeing job security.

How can these principles be continuously reinforced through the in-plant culture? It is done through the material culture of objects, through daily routine activities, through repetition of acts that symbolize shared meanings, and through the language that is used to describe things.

Almost everyone who has written about life inside the transplants has noted the response of American workers to the surface level of equality that characterizes plant ambiance: "We dress, park, eat, and live together" (Hill et al. 1989:80). "Everyone at the Flat Rock plant would be called by their first name: Mazda did not allow 'misters.' There would be no reserved spots for managers in the plant parking lot, and no executive dining room, as there were in American plants" (Fucini and Fucini 1990:3). An interview with a Japanese associate employed in a transplant mirrors the comments of American workers:

> Executives don't have private offices and their desks are located in a common open space. Neither do they have special parking lot spaces or private dining rooms. It is rather hard for American managers to accept this idea because they lose the privileges they had become accustomed to before coming to work for U.S. transplants. This idea fosters good communication among all employees.

And Cornfield (1989) describes attending a business executive award ceremony at which a Nissan CEO received his award in the same blue jumpsuit worn by production workers and management.

Uniforms worn by all employees (though not compulsory at all plants) from trainees to executives are a powerful symbol of equality, as is the use of single terms like *associates* to refer to all production employees. The spirit of openness and teamwork is symbolized in the organization of administrative areas. Desks of all managers are arranged in rows without dividers. Private space is the exception, and is used primarily for conferences. Critics of the effort to build an egalitarian culture often refer to the uniforms, common dining facilities, and the like as superficial or surface culture. But all elements of material culture are superficial in the sense that they do not tell the observer about how those who wear the uniforms or eat in the same dining room feel about these things. One must look for broader culture patterns, comprised of the separate elements, that form the basis of the shared meanings and a common understanding that constitute culture.

Some companies, like Toyota, are attempting to create the broader culture patterns and to make the transplant become a small society. At its plant site in Georgetown, Kentucky, Toyota is constructing a financial center, day care center, health and recreation facility, and social center. They are very large structures using advanced architectural designs, and they look more like a resort than an auto plant. Such facilities will tend to blur the boundaries between work, family, and community. Spouses and children of transplant workers will use these facilities for everyday life activities, and they will be involved with other workers and their families. Nissan is also at work creating an image of benevolence with a fitness center, two swimming pools, tennis courts, softball fields, a running trail, horseshoe pits, and picnic areas. And it is not only fun and games that Nissan provides to create the culture of concern for employees. Workers can lease Nissan cars and trucks at a discount, with the insurance and maintenance provided by the company.

All of these things, viewed separately, may be superficial, but at the very least they provide a powerful set of incentives for transplant workers to want to hold on to their jobs.

Throughout this section and previous sections we have relied on some of the things that workers say about their employers as a way of gauging their feelings about working in a transplant. We should approach these statements with caution since they have been made to reporters or researchers in situations where anonymity cannot be guaranteed. The following statement was made by one autoworker to a reporter who was trying to learn from workers how they felt about working in a Japanese transplant:

> You're not going to get an accurate picture of this because everybody will lie because they're scared of losing their jobs. They just do as they please in there. The union is in the pocket of management. You don't want this in Kentucky. This sucks. (*Lexington Herald-Leader*, April 23, 1986)

TRANSPLANTING STRUCTURE AND BUILDING A WORKPLACE CULTURE: IS IT TAKING HOLD?

The efforts by the transplants to create a new worker involve both a new production system, or a way of doing work, and a new way of thinking about oneself as a worker and community member. The new production system involves changing what people do in direct production activities, and changing how indirect activities in support of production are organized. Direct production activity takes place in teams of multiskilled workers who are expected to participate in rationalizing their own work. Many indirect workers' jobs such as inspection, repair, and maintenance have been eliminated, and the responsibilities incorporated into the teams.

The reduction of job classifications and creation of multiskilled workers is facilitated by jobs being rotated among team members. Rotation is also designed to reduce injuries and stress associated with the work pace and repetitive motion tasks (Florida and Kenney 1991). Materials needed in the production process are provided by a new system of suppliers whose proximity to the transplant facilitates the just-in-time control of inventory, whereby parts are not provided to workers until they are needed.

The Japanese system of organizing work in the transplants has been studied extensively by Richard Florida and Martin Kenney. In a summary of their research findings they conclude that "the findings of our research. . .provide ample evidence that in the old fordist industries the Japanese transplants are successfully transferring the basic elements of the Japanese production system to the United States" (Kenney and Florida 1993:8). Their conclusion is based on research findings that auto transplant firms and their suppliers follow similar approaches in selecting and training workers, in using work teams, in reducing the number of job classifications, and in encouraging worker involvement.

Kenney and Florida see in Japanese industrial organization a new model of production that is unrivaled in its potential for productivity and high work commitment. They refer to the model as "innovation-mediated production," containing five components: emphasis on mental skills, collective intelligence as represented by teamwork, rapid pace of technological innovation, continuous improvement in the work process, and closer ties between research and development and the factory floor. Although the authors claim that their model is not synonymous with the Japanese system, the elements of their model are not so much theoretically derived, as extensions of empirical conditions in Japanese firms.

One of the central features of Japanese industrial organization is the work team, and there are different views of its effectiveness. Womack et al. (1990) view the team as a key element of "lean production" because it is the location for efficient production and improvements in the work process. The team is self-directed, with team leaders who function as workers and coordinators, and who also fill in for absent workers. As they state:

So in the end, it is the dynamic work team that emerges as the heart of the lean factory. Building these efficient teams is not simple. First, workers need to be taught a wide variety of skills—in fact, all the jobs in their work group so that tasks can be rotated and workers can fill in for each other. Workers then need to acquire many additional skills: simple machine repair, quality-checking, housekeeping, and materials ordering. Then they need encouragement to think *proactively*, so they can devise solutions before problems become serious. (p. 99)

As noted in Chapter 1, Berggren and his associates (1991; Berggren 1992) are less sanguine about the work team. They do not see the same level of skill involved in the jobs of team members, and they see the team concept as reflecting the absence of labor-management antagonism rather than worker self-management. Berggren suggests that the Japanese concept of work group might be better translated as "platoon" rather than as "team" (Berggren 1992:48).

The strengths of Japanese industrial organization are acknowledged by Berggren (1992) and summarized to be:

1. their greater commitment to job security,
2. their egalitarian appearance,
3. their attention to work at the shop-floor level,
4. their emphasis on quality and pride in work, and
5. their careful selection of workers.

Disadvantages are found in

1. the speed and intensity of work,
2. the expansion of work time and the expectation that workers will stay when needed,
3. the potential for physical and mental health risks, and
4. the hegemonic nature of the factory regime, reflected in uniforms, detailed regulations, conduct, and discipline codes.

Womack et al. (1990) disagree with those who see stress and tension in lean production, arguing that critics misunderstand the difference between tension and the challenges associated with solving problems with their own skills. They refer to the latter as a "creative tension," which gives workers control over their own work. With respect to work-related injuries, Kenney and Florida (1993) claimed that they may be due to the failure to fully use the Japanese system. Job rotation is designed to offset the problems of repetitive motion jobs, and it may not be implemented as frequently in the transplants as it is in Japan.

It might be safe to conclude that the structure of Japanese industrial organization has been successfully transplanted, but it is difficult to know if the effort to create a new worker and a new workplace culture is taking hold. There have been no studies based on large samples of transplant workers revealing how they respond to Japanese management philosophy and the team approach to work. We must rely on evidence of support for the Japanese system or of opposition or resistance to the new culture as it is reported in case studies, in interviews with selected workers, or in newspaper accounts of in-plant life.

Let us consider the company uniform to start with. The uniform is a material symbol of common affiliation with a company. Presumably if you identify with the company you will not resent being expected to wear its uniform. Relevant to this point is a study of soldiers in World War II that found the best indicator of a soldier's satisfaction with the army was whether the soldier wore the uniform, rather than civilian clothes, during off-base leaves (Stouffer 1943).

When the author toured the SIA plant he estimated that the majority of workers were wearing the full uniform. The remainder wore either the company shirt with jeans, or the uniform pants with a T-shirt. Only a handful of workers wore neither the shirt nor pants of the uniform. All employees wore white hard hats, which had the red-white-and-blue SIA logo in front. At least one worker was making what I interpret to be a statement of opposition by wearing his hard hat backwards with an American flag decal on the back of the hat. There was also reported resistance to Mazda's effort to get workers to wear a company baseball cap with the mandatory uniform (Fucini and Fucini 1990:104). The dispute was whether wearing the cap was voluntary or mandatory. It was resolved to mean voluntary, resulting in most workers going capless.

There is also evidence from research at Mazda and Subaru-Isuzu that Japanese management philosophy, as presented during recruitment and training sessions, starts to break down under the pressure of full production (Fucini and Fucini 1990:Chapter 9; Graham 1991:Chapter 7). Worker input and participation disappeared and were replaced by unilateral decisions by team leaders or by management decisions to program detailed steps in the work process in a manner reminiscent of Fordism. At best, team discussions to solve problems became exercises in manipulating group consensus on plans already devised by management.

*Kaizen*ing for continuous improvement became efforts to squeeze seconds out of every production cycle until workers were moving continuously from car to car without as much as a five-second break. Enthusiasm for discussion of how to eliminate waste and inefficiency declined as it became apparent that *kaizen* was a way to increase the workload.

Thus, there is evidence that workers at the transplants are not fully enthusiastic about uniforms, exercise sessions, and a variety of slogans

and rituals. There is also evidence of disappointment concerning promises made in recruitment and training about a new kind of management
and worker that were not being realized in the workplace. However, in
contrast to this evidence we know that attempts at unionizing workers at
several of the transplants have not been successful. In 1985 a union-
organizing effort at Honda was canceled by the union just prior to a
scheduled election. In 1989, an election was held at Nissan and the United
Auto Workers union was defeated 1,622 to 718, with almost all of the
2,400 workers voting.

The defeat of these unionizing efforts is undoubtedly due in part to the
intense opposition provided by Honda and Nissan. Both companies supported "spontaneous" antiunion committees formed by workers at both
plants with intensive campaigns that raised worker fears about job loss if
the union should win. But the failure of the unionizing effort was probably also due in part to justifiable worker fears about the past failure of
unions to protect jobs in the totally unionized Big Three U.S. auto firms.

It is not clear what the union defeat tells us about how workers feel
about working at Honda or Nissan. Workers were acting and voting
against something—the uncertainty associated with having a union. They
were not necessarily voting for an endorsement of the policies and practices of their employers.

There is better evidence about how people in at least one community
feel about their new corporate citizen. As noted in Chapter 1, interviews
with central Kentucky residents by a university research group between
1986 and 1990 were conducted to assess the public's views of Toyota
(Houghland 1991). These surveys indicate that Toyota's image as a corporate citizen is overwhelmingly positive, and they are confident that
Toyota will fulfill its obligations to the community.

The existence of strong positive sentiments in the general community
would seem to reinforce the image of shared interests and trust between
community and corporation, and these sentiments will no doubt influence the way that workers think about their bonds with a corporation that
they work with and not simply work for.

The quoted statements at the start of this chapter by transplant executives in Indiana, Kentucky, and Tennessee are an integral part of the
messages transmitted to the community and workers in the recruitment,
selection, and training programs of the transplants. The crucial test of this
effort to create a new worker and a new corporation-community relationship will be the corporation's ability to fulfill the promise of job security,
even in tough economic times. That is, after all, the promise of the Japanese auto firms that sets them apart from U.S. automakers. There is some
evidence to indicate that Nissan went to great lengths to avoid layoffs
despite the buildup of inventory (Gelsanliter 1992). However, this oc-

curred during a union-organizing drive and may have been done to illustrate Nissan's commitment to job security.

A more interesting industrywide approach to even out production and avoid layoffs is reflected in an effort by Toyota and Honda to export U.S.-made cars to Japan, Taiwan, Europe, and the Middle East (*New York Times*, March 25, 1993, p. A1). Japanese auto plants in the United States, Europe, and Japan can balance their total production in a way that permits gradual reduction in daily output, rather than sharply reducing production when there is industry buildup. This avoids having to lay off workers.

It is, of course, too soon to know if the transplants will be able to keep their implicit commitment to job security. There is some evidence that workers at transplants believe that they have job security, often because of the employment of several hundred temporary workers who can be laid off if there is a slowdown. And there is some evidence that management supports job security because it produces a more "dependent" employee. The president of Nissan in Tennessee stated: "To guarantee employment and livelihood of employees will enhance their sense of dependence on the group, which in turn will develop their sense of loyalty and belonging" (*Murfreesboro Daily News Journal*, April 27, 1981).

If job security for workers in transplants is an official and operative goal of the Japanese firms studied in this book, it is simultaneously a commitment to the state and community that provided the public resources needed by the transplants. This may, in fact, be the beginnings of a new direction in economic life, one that is based on fairness, democracy, and community. Or it may simply be business as usual, with large corporations using a new way to gain the cooperation of government and labor while they pursue their basic goal of profit.

Chapter 6

In the Heart of the Heart of the Country: Corporatism as Civic Virtue

In the course of reading some high school essays to determine the winner of an essay entitled "Tennessee and Japan," I noticed that some of the high school students were saying, "the two countries," meaning Tennessee and Japan. At first I thought that this was some kind of an error that someone had made. They are just high school students. Then I realized that they were really interpreting a new phenomenon in that Tennessee was acting very much like a country in its direct relationships with Japan.
                —Director, Japan Center of Tennessee

Let us take a moment to recapitulate. Up to this point we have done several things. First, we provided an account of the global and local economic conditions that gave rise to the actions of Japanese automobile companies to locate new assembly plants in the United States. Next, we examined the question of why six Japanese firms chose to locate where they did, and identified those factors that seem to distinguish states with transplants from other states that were unsuccessful competitors. Third, we looked at how the transplants went about selecting their work force from among tens of thousand of applicants, and how that process may have produced a work force with special commitments to their organizations. And fourth, we analyzed newspaper coverage of the transplant projects, which revealed an emphasis on the benefits of the transplants and representation of the views of political and business elites rather than a balance of views.

Much of the above has to do with the practice and ideology of corporatism—the actions of government and business to bring the transplant to their states, and the characterization of those actions as a new cooperative effort to benefit all segments of the community. In this chapter we turn to the second stage of the transplant project: the process by

125

which transplants, once in place, are more fully integrated into the social and cultural system of a community.

The structure and ideology of corporatism achieves its credibility through the way that people in the community think about and talk about the transplant. The way that people are influenced to think about transplants is by the penetration of the ideology of corporatism into the social networks, interest groups, and voluntary associations that make up the community. We refer to this penetration as the process of *embeddedness*, or the way that a collection of beliefs about the transplant project finds its way into business groups, labor unions, schools, religious groups, and cultural groups. A focus on the process of embeddedness will allow us to see how economic actions, such as the transplant project, are shaped by social and organizational relations that can have an independent impact on an economic system.

In this chapter we try to illustrate the importance of the social side of economic activity (i.e., embeddedness) by (1) examining views of the transplant project from persons in different community sectors, (2) analyzing the sociological (as compared to financial) significance of states' economic incentive packages, and (3) studying the way that noneconomic community groups are drawn into projects that provide the concrete personal and organizational ties that are supportive of the transplant project.

REACTIONS TO THE TRANSPLANT PROJECT: POLITICS, BUSINESS, LABOR

Representatives from different sectors of the community provide diverse views on the new corporate citizen in their community. Political leaders and those affiliated with the business community tend to be very positive, while representatives of labor and environmental groups are more cautious or negative about the project.

One mayor of a transplant community could see nothing negative about the entire project. He was asked if there was any controversy or disagreement about the state's incentive package, or the idea of bringing in a foreign firm:

> There was no real opposition. There was one "crank," that's what I would call him, who was concerned about the environment. I think he just wanted publicity. We didn't give away anything. This is the best deal anyone could ever get. I would do it all over again if given the chance. We didn't give any tax abatements. We put up some money for the training and extended utilities because the plant was included in city limits.

The mayor's recall of events reflecting opposition is selective, as there was more than one "crank" who took a public position against the transplant project or the incentive package. The mayor is correct in stating that his city did not give any tax abatements, but he fails to mention that the city put up $500,000 for additional police and fire protection and that the county issued a $500 million revenue bond and made a commitment to build two new high schools at a projected cost of $24 million. The mayor was asked if there were any negative outcomes from a large development project like the transplant:

> Half of the plant's employees already live in the county. So if we have problems, then we had them before the plant came. Some say there has been an impact on schools. That's not so. Our town was growing before the plant came and we just continued.

In an effort to see if the mayor could see anything other than benefits associated with the project, we discussed the question of surplus production in the auto industry, especially in the states in his region. He was asked what he thought might happen if the plant had to cut back production:

> They never slow down or cut back. The interesting thing is they cut production in their plants in Japan but not here. We have a real safety net that we never expected.

Another mayor was more succinct in his response but he was equally unequivocal in his positive view. How did he feel about the transplant project?

> The high point of my career as mayor has been this project. It required an extraordinary cooperative effort between units of government and it has been very rewarding.

The very positive views of elected officials responsible for negotiating some aspects of the incentive package are understandable, given that they are on the hot seat with regard to any local complaints about the new plant. Business leaders from Kentucky, on the other hand, could perhaps more easily afford to recognize some of the problems brought by the transplant while still being very supportive. On the question of opposition to the transplant project:

> We had some opposition here. The dispute with labor is fake. They just wanted a share of the construction jobs. Some of the downtown business people are concerned about the fringe development that will bring malls

and K-Mart. And then there was opposition to any kind of change by the "old boys." But we are handling all of this with a lot of planning and working together. There is a real sense of partnership in our community.

What about possible negative outcomes from a project like this, things that might not have been anticipated in advance and that might be seen as inevitable in any growth situation?

Well there has been the increase in traffic, but that's all relative. Housing became a problem because we overbuilt high-cost units for the management types. We need more multiunit housing. We also need to get our high schools up to snuff.

Kentucky business leaders were also more sensitive to and realistic about the matter of business slowdown. What would happen if Toyota had to cut back production?

Any cutback would be hard for us. It would harm us because of the drop in tax revenue. Let's be honest, most firms are not real community citizens. We hope to get there, but not yet. Toyota has the potential to become a real community citizen. Most firms leave in a minute when things are bad. But can something the size of Toyota leave? Toyota is a good citizen, but they just don't give. They want to be asked. That gives them control.

This sense of optimism and partnership is not shared by community leaders outside of the business sector, and their views are less often heard (as we learned from our analysis of newspapers in Chapter 4). The views of a local union official do not give the same sense of community reported above. What did he think about the matter of controversy or disagreement about the state's incentive package, or the idea of bringing in a foreign firm?

There was no organized continuing opposition. Labor does meet periodically to discuss issues, but no one is really looking at the impact of these transplants. The Blue Grass Tomorrow group is trying to preserve the character of this part of the world without stopping everything. They're a pretty establishment group. It's not little old ladies worried about toxic waste, but the economic elites.
Q. Are you optimistic about the efforts to build partnerships between government, corporations, and labor?
A. We are not part of the partnership. Labor is on the outside looking in. We are not a player. We have been coopted and given lip service. We have been excluded from all the manufacturing projects that have followed Toyota. They are part of the *keiretsu* of suppliers and labor has been frozen out.

The labor official was asked his views of the long-term impact of the transplant project. What would be its effect on the city or state in the years ahead?

The Toyota project looked like an economic development project at the beginning, but it has resulted in a transformation of the way that business is done. It has been taken out of the hands of local elected officials and new decision-makers are in charge. We have yet to get a picture of the true costs of the Toyota project. If we could get those numbers I think it would be staggering to most people. It's tough getting the attention of people in Kentucky because Toyota has brought jobs and money. But the big picture is awful. The Japanese are interesting and congenial people. But when you get an organized group of them, they are awesome competitors.

Representatives of local environmental organizations were interviewed and they reported a good working relationship with Toyota, but they did not seem to feel that it amounted to very much. In July 1988 the Land and Nature Trust of the Bluegrass ran ads in the *Lexington Herald-Leader* that were critical of the growth of heavy industry in this area. What was the impact of those ads?

[Person 1] After we ran those ads Toyota was more eager to establish relations with us. Toyota initiated the contact with us and asked us to send representatives to meet with their staff.
[Person 2] Land and Nature Trust goes out there [Toyota plant] four times a year to meet with their head of the environmental control unit. He updates us on all the problems at Toyota and the things they are doing to watch their effluent. I think our meetings are useful, but in reality we have no leverage.

There is another interesting aspect to the way that political and business leaders respond to the Japanese transplants. Business and political leaders who have been involved with the Japanese executives in negotiating some part of the incentive package invariably have a story about the Japanese that serves to humanize the relationship between a multinational corporation and a local community. I call them "mom and pop" stories because they give the impression that decisions involving hundreds of millions of dollars seem to turn on small human events that have nothing to do with business or economics.

A university official who was involved in negotiations with the Japanese about the university's role in in-plant training, language programs, and cultural education describes a site visit by the Japanese while the interstate competition was still in process.

Early in the negotiations they sent their top people. They wanted to see a non-union manufacturing plant. I talked them into visiting —————— because of their special management approach. We went there for what was to be a half-hour visit. Two workers were invited to the meeting and the Japanese spent three hours talking to them. They were fascinated by the fact that both workers still had small farms that they worked, and that they wanted to stay on the land and not move to the city. This meant something to the Japanese. They have special feelings about the land. [He then describes the Shinto ceremony at the plant opening and the rituals involving the soil— shoveling it around, throwing it in the air.] I think the Japanese were also concerned about one of the competing sites being "dry." They wanted to go shopping at the mall. We walked around looking at the shops until we saw a package store. They went in and bought a bottle of bourbon, then we left.

Another mom and pop story is provided by the director of an economic development group involved with recruiting foreign firms to the community. He tells the story of a Japanese CEO on a site visit who is playing golf with J. R. Smith, the CEO of a local industrial firm:

While they were playing golf the Japanese CEO started to get some vision problems. We didn't know it, but he detached his retina while hitting a ball. I took him to an eye doctor who said this man needs surgery today or he could lose his vision. I called J. R. and told him the problem. He said, "Tom it's time to go to battle stations." J. R.'s on the board at Mayo, and that afternoon our visitor was on J. R.'s corporate jet to Mayo. Everything worked out fine and don't you think that story didn't make the rounds in Japan.

A final account is provided by the mayor of a transplant city who is a World War II veteran with extensive involvement in the Pacific theater. He was trying to impress on the interviewer that World War II was over, and that he harbored no animosity toward the Japanese. His account involves the local transplant president and the CEO of the parent firm from Japan:

We had a three-way meeting to discuss some plans for expansion. Billings [president of the local transplant] and the top CEO from Japan were trying to get my reactions to their plans for future development of the plant. After the meeting, Billings came by and asked me what I thought of his boss. I told him "I think I recognized the son of a bitch—he dropped one of the bombs on Pearl Harbor."

The above reported perceptions of the Japanese and of the transplant project convey several things. First is a genuine respect for the Japanese as business people, to be taken seriously and as formidable competitors. Second is a genuine affection for individuals from Japan that they have met, negotiated with, and may still continue to work with. Some of the community leaders who we interviewed also give the impression that their relations with the Japanese are part business and part human relations. The transplant project is sometimes described as if it were solely an opportunity to enrich the community through greater cultural diversity. If there is anything that seems to provoke a uniform response among community leaders is any suggestion of Japan bashing or racism on the part of the community's rednecks.

INCENTIVE PACKAGES

Most discussion of the incentive packages provided by states to the transplants is concerned with its economic meaning. How much? For what purpose? How long will it take to get it back? Did we provide more than was necessary? Most of the public discussion of the transplants, and the basis for whatever criticism develops, is focused on the incentives. For example, gubernatorial campaigns in two transplant states found the out-of-power party candidates being very critical of the state "giveaways" in the incentive packages. After being elected, both of the new governors played down their concerns about incentives and pledged to honor the agreements negotiated by the prior administrations.

But there is another story to be explored about the incentive packages. One that has less to do with money, because the money may not be the most important thing to the Japanese corporations. The absolute dollar value of each state's incentive package is on the order of 5 to 15 percent of the total investment by the Japanese firm. The size of each firm's capital investment is so large that it could easily have absorbed the additional costs of the incentive package, if it were not available. In fact, a Toyota official has suggested that discussion of incentives may follow rather than precede the location decision. Consider the following interview with a Japanese CEO reported in the *Louisville Courier-Journal*:

Q. How critical to your decision was the $125 million incentive package the state offered?
A. That cancelled out certain disadvantages that the state had. It enabled us to put Kentucky on the same list as other states.
Q. Did other states offer more than $125 million?
A. I cannot say because once we actually decided to come here then we started to go into details. The other states we did not get into that. Those incentives [from Kentucky] were just enough to cancel out the disadvantages, such as inadequate sewage capacity, hilly land and narrow roads near the site. If the government had not offered that we would not have been able to come here. But we came here not because of that (the incentive package)

but because we felt we had the full support of the people here. (October 14, 1986, p. B12)

What else is there about the incentive package that may be of interest to Japanese investors? Consider first of all the fact that states report that Japanese firms insist that all negotiations about the plant site and incentives be carried out in secret. The Bloomington, Illinois, city manager who negotiated with Mitsubishi and Chrysler discussed the problem of carrying out negotiations while complying with the state's Open Meetings Act, which requires any meeting of two or more elected officials to be open to the public (Dirks 1992). So what did they do? They honored the letter of the law but not the spirit:

> We had to find a way to communicate without breaking the law. We did this with individual communication and memorandum. It was awkward to work with, not ideal. It also created problems with the press, causing a lot of strained relations. We pride ourselves with being very open and honest. It was very uncomfortable.

In the case of Nissan in Tennessee, it is reported that the governor invited the leadership of Rutherford County (proposed site of the transplant) to his mansion, not to his office because then it would have been a public meeting. Similarly, in Ohio, the discussion of Honda's interest in a plant site was kept from newspapers and local business associations (Gelsanliter 1992:25, 50).

One mayor of a city with a transplant said that although he honored the request of the Japanese for secrecy in the early negotiations he never did understand the reason for it:

> I think the secrecy stuff was a joke. We were not supposed to have any public discussion of the possibility of them coming, and we were supposed to keep it out of the papers. But then a site visit team would visit and there would be no effort to stay out of public view. One time we were meeting with a group of Japanese about what we would do for site preparation. They wanted to take a break and go out to one of the malls. So there we are, me, some of my staff and a bunch of Japanese walking around in the mall. Well, lots of people know me in town and they would come over to shake hands and invariably ask if we were working on a new Japanese plant. Not much secrecy in that.

The insistence on secrecy by local and state officials at the time that they are discussing the details of a proposed incentive package would seem to be and probably is impossible. But perhaps the purpose of the secrecy dictum is to see if there is any significant opposition to the transplant project. If a local group of political or business leaders were unhappy about bringing a foreign firm with tax money they would certainly blow the whistle on the secret negotiations. It would not only expose opposition, but would also show whether the opposition can get the support of local or state media outlets in exposing the irregularities.

Once discussion of the incentive package plan leaves the inner circle of political and business leaders and is presented to the public, there is a second opportunity to assess the strength of support or opposition. Typically, the first public announcement of the project has the status of a proposal rather than a done deal. Consider, for example, the following sequence of 1980 front-page headlines from the *Murfreesboro Daily News Journal* beginning with the first mention of the Nissan plant and Smyrna, Tennessee:

> Ridley Believes Datsun Coming (September 18)
> County to Begin Talks With Datsun Officials (September 19)
> Project Finds Quick Support (September 20)
> Talks With Nissan Important to All (editorial, September 21)
> Nissan Session Held (September 22)
> Nissan Corp. Wants To Be Wanted (September 23)
> Funding For Nissan Discussed (September 25)
> County Doesn't Have the Inside Track: Nissan (September 26)

Such headlines continued almost daily until October 30, when the headline was "Nissan Coming To Rutherford." Thus, there was almost a six-week period during which matters related to state and local incentives, the plant site, and Nissan's needs were presented to the people of Rutherford County and beyond. If there were to be substantial opposition to the project from any sector of the community it should have begun to surface.

The potential for political debate in each state over the incentive package provides the Japanese decision-makers with an indication of the strength of the political and economic coalition supporting the incentive plan. A governor who makes promises to the Japanese in private will not be very credible if he or she is faced with daily criticism from opponents to the project. Similarly, a legislature or business community that is seriously divided on the incentive initiative will not be viewed as a favorable site location regardless of the dollar value of the incentives. Such states engender greater unpredictability about the future with regard to pro-business and progrowth programs, and thus are unattractive sites for a transplant.

If we expand this situation to include three or four states that are competing for a transplant, we can see how a firm looking for a site would benefit. Each competing state, operating with a pledge of secrecy, develops an incentive package with the assistance of political officials and business leaders. Each makes its plan available to the public, indicating that its state or city is one of several being considered as the location for an auto assembly plant. While this is going on, the firm trying to select a site can assess the value of the incentives that each state may provide and the strength of a state's or community's commitment to the project. In this way, the politics of the incentive package may be more important than its economics.

EMBEDDEDNESS: THE SOCIAL SIDE OF ECONOMIC ACTIVITY

At the beginning of Chapter One we described the intense pressure that was put on the Japanese in 1980 to do something about their success in gaining market share in the United States. Calls from political officials, labor, and the Big Three automakers for the Japanese to reduce their exports or face stiff quotas led to the reluctant decision by the Japanese to build assembly plants in the United States. This was a painful lesson for the Japanese, but they learned how important it is to have a favorable and supportive value climate to reinforce one's economic objectives. They saw how public demonstrations by unemployed autoworkers translated into political pressure in Congress and to support for legislation setting limits on Japanese auto imports.

In order to help create a favorable value climate for Japanese investment in the United States, the National Association of Japan-America Societies (NAJAS) was formed in 1979. As a nonprofit national organization, NAJAS provides support to a cooperative network of independent Japan-America Societies located throughout the United States. As of December, 1992 twenty-five state Japan-America Societies were members of NAJAS. The mission of NAJAS

> is to strengthen and support the initiatives of its member-societies, facilitate communication between societies, and promote the exchange and sharing of ideas, information and program resources. NAJAS develops programs, offers program implementation assistance, and consults with member-societies on a variety of administrative issues. In addition, NAJAS assists and advises newly forming societies, and coordinates an annual national conference of Japan-America Societies. (NAJAS, no date:3)

From the fall of 1989 through the fall of 1991, NAJAS sponsored thirty-seven programs of lectures, performances, films, and panels in cities across the United States to improve understanding of the United States, Japan, and their interrelationships.

Interviews with directors of Japan-America Societies in the states with auto transplants indicate that they are involved in promoting a variety of activities that provide a forum for exchange between people of the state and Japan. The activities include luncheons and dinners with speakers, sports events, cultural festivals, business and educational programs, and family-related social events.

One director reported that the state society is very active, sponsoring ten events in 1992, twenty in 1991, and fifteen in 1990. The cost of these activities is supported by the membership fees of 150 corporate members, both Japanese and American firms. The director said, "The American firms usually have business ties with Japan or Japanese firms in the U.S." Corporate members with more than one hundred employees pay $1,200 per year; those with twenty to ninety-nine employees pay $600; and those with fewer than twenty employees pay $240. Nonprofit organizations can become members for $120 and individuals for $50 per year. The society has thirty-one persons on its board of directors: eight from industry, six from law firms, five from educational institutions, four from banking, and the remainder from business associations, utilities, or state agencies.

Another JAS director reported that their society had 120 corporate members, about 60 percent Japanese and 40 percent U.S. firms. There are about 90 wholly owned or joint venture Japanese firms in the state and two-thirds belong to the state society. We discussed the main focus of the society's work in the state:

My predecessor worked primarily on cultural events. My focus has been to be a business liaison between Japanese and American business. I do a number of things to get them to know each other and learn how to do business together. We have weekly cocktail parties around the state which works well as an informal way to bring business people together.

Although their focus is on business relations, they still get involved with cultural events:

We brought the Kodo drummers, which we cosponsored with the Center for the Arts. We are working on a mobile exhibit to send to schools around the state. It will contain audiovisuals on Japanese history and culture. And we get involved in activities that do not focus on Japan or the transplant. Our chairman is on the board of the National Council of Christians and Jews and he is interested in developing a multicultural program.

Another director of a Japan-America Society pointed out that many activities related to Japan take place throughout the state quite independently of the society:

There are very active groups around the state that develop their own programs without any relationship with me. I communicate with them via a
newsletter and help if I can. Japanese firms in the state do many things to
integrate Japanese into the community and to present programs on the
culture and history of Japan. These groups do not need the state Japan-
America Society.

The activities of the Japan-America Societies throughout the United
States are a way of drawing upon many noneconomic groups in a community to provide a supportive context for a variety of relationships
between Japanese and American society. Civic, cultural, religious, and
educational groups are brought together to build a climate of understanding and cooperation between the people of two countries. In Chapter 1 we
referred to these activities as examples of *embeddedness*, a process by
which social relationships between people and groups have an impact on
economic life. In this way the new partnerships between Japanese auto
firms, state governments, and local communities are supported and facilitated by social relations that are not economic in nature or purpose.
Community programs on Japanese culture and history provide knowledge and a positive feeling about Japan. This positive feeling can carry
over to favorable views of joint economic ventures between U.S. and
Japanese firms. In a more direct way, social contacts and friendships
between Japanese and American business people that are formed at a
museum exhibit of Japanese art may provide the incentive for a business
transaction that might otherwise not have occurred.

Local communities that are the sites of the transplants may also have an
interest in building a climate of understanding that will make Japanese
executives and their wives and children feel welcome in the community.
Political and business leaders who may have been involved in formulat-
ing the community's role in the incentive package will be concerned about
how the community will receive its new members. One economic development official described his idea for an "aftercare program" for the new
Japanese companies that are recruited to the community. This involves
organizing social events for new families, getting local families to serve as
"contacts" for the wives and children from Japan, and to do what is
needed to facilitate integration into community life.

But embeddedness will not be found in all transplant communities. It is
not an official program, and it is not part of the incentive package that can
be carried out like a revenue bond or a worker selection program. Embeddedness is facilitated or impeded by certain conditions in a community.
We theorize that there are three main sources of variation in embeddedness. The first source involves the extent of concern by the transplant's
top management with a community's receptivity to the transplant. If top

management is Japanese, and the plant has a large contingent of Japanese managers and their families, there will be greater interest in achieving a smooth integration into the community. The fact that transplants are located in small communities increases the visibility of the new residents and their concern with harmonious relations.

The second factor that will produce variation in embeddedness is the degree to which a community's business class is organized and unified in support of the transplant project. Organization of the business class is reflected in the strength of associations such as the Chamber of Commerce or the existence of private-sector development groups committed to growth and to attracting new firms to the community. A unified business class will also support the use of local incentives (e.g., tax abatement, land development) for new firms and will not see such expenditures as competing with the needs of local firms. In some communities, local business may not be supportive of foreign firms or multinationals because they often drive up wages or because they are viewed as not being committed to the community in the same way as locally owned firms. Our hypothesis is that intrabusiness class conflict about the transplant will limit the extent and effectiveness of the embeddedness process.

The final local condition that is expected to limit or enhance the embeddedness process is the strength of organized public opposition to the corporatist project. Preliminary examination of the six transplant communities reveals important variations in the extent and strength of opposition to the project, and the particular time in the project's phase that the opposition occurs. For example, the case of the Toyota plant in Georgetown, Kentucky, reveals considerable organized public opposition in the year preceding the actual opening of the plant. There was organized opposition in public meetings, demonstrations, and the courts, coming from the small-business community, environmentalists, and labor (see Chapter Four for discussion of the opposition).

In contrast, the case of the Subaru-Isuzu plant in Indiana reveals little or no public opposition to the plant in the year prior to its opening. The only major public controversy occurred after the plant opened and was an instance of symbolic or cultural conflict, rather than conflict about the incentive package, the quality of life in the community, or the rights of labor. The conflict (discussed in Chapter 4) involves opposition by a local veteran's group to the city's proposal to change the name of a street in a city park to Ota City Drive. The city's proposal was part of a sister city relationship, and the veterans' opposition was that the renamed street was near a veterans' memorial in the park. After the veterans' public challenge to the mayor at a Memorial Day ceremony in the park, the renaming proposal was withdrawn.

In between the case of Toyota in Kentucky and Subaru-Isuzu in Indiana is Nissan in Tennessee, where a moderate amount of opposition to the transplant took place. The first sign of opposition was three weeks after Nissan said they were coming to Smyrna, when the County Farm Bureau went on record against the plant because of the expected increase in land values that would make it difficult to use land for farming. The second instance of opposition was when fifty citizens proposed giving a new road being built to serve Nissan the name Pearl Harbor Highway. The third case of opposition involved a public protest by labor unions at the Nissan ground-breaking ceremony. The protests were over the selection of a nonunion construction firm to build the plant. None of these instances of opposition were as enduring as in the Kentucky-Toyota case, and none reached the level of court actions to actually try to derail the project.

In summary, we have identified three factors that can produce variations in how the process of embeddedness develops in a transplant community: (1) the interest of top management, (2) unified or divided business class, and (3) strength of opposition to the transplant. If we apply these three factors to the experiences of the host communities in Indiana, Kentucky, and Tennessee we can offer an hypothesis about where we expect embeddedness to be strongest.

Table 6.1 shows how these factors apply across the three states. Indiana has Japanese top management (which we assume means they are more interested in community integration), no public opposition to the project from the business class, and very weak public opposition to the project. Thus we predict that there will be a strong effort to push embeddedness in the community. In contrast, we expect a weak effort to push embeddedness in Kentucky, because there is a divided business community and strong opposition to the transplant project. Kentucky does have Japanese management, but their assumed interest in integration will not have the

Table 6.1. Factors Related to Embeddedness in Indiana, Kentucky, and Tennessee

	Top management	Organization of business class	Organized opposition	Prediction on embeddedness
Indiana (Subaru-Isuzu)	Japanese	Unified	Weak	Effective effort
Kentucky (Toyota)	Japanese	Divided	Strong	Ineffective effort
Tennessee (Nissan)	American	Unified (except Farm Bureau)	Moderate	Moderately effective effort

full support of the community. Tennessee has American top management and therefore should be less committed to cultural integration. It has a moderately unified business class and a moderate degree of organized opposition to the transplant project. We therefore expect a moderate effort to push the embeddedness process.

Let us now look at each state to see if our predictions on embeddedness are supported. We looked for evidence of embeddedness from data obtained from interviews and from newspaper accounts that point to the existence of community projects in the cultural, educational, and religious subcommunities. These projects would be directed toward furthering exchange and understanding between Japanese and American people, and would therefore provide indirect support for the transplant initiative.

EMBEDDEDNESS IN INDIANA: PERSONAL AND ORGANIZATIONAL RELATIONSHIPS

We now turn to evidence of embeddedness in the way that the structure and ideology of corporatism, which is the basis of the transplant project, penetrate a variety of local groups. We examine activities of a variety of community groups that are drawn into cooperative projects that can provide tacit support for the idea of growth embodied by the transplants. Some of the activities and programs that we examine were initiated by Subaru-Isuzu and some by local business groups.

In the educational sector, there are seven distinct programs that involve local organizations and groups. Primary and secondary schools have participated in teacher and student travel programs to Japan during summer months, supported with funds from the auto transplant and private foundations. Vocational programs in area high schools and technology training centers received a total of forty-four pickup trucks from the transplant for use in their courses. The local university has sponsored a lecture series and an interest group seminar on topics related to Japanese society involving faculty, students, members of the local community, and auto executives. The university also created a Pacific Rim Initiative, which consisted of recruiting new faculty to teach courses on Chinese and Japanese languages, and a small grants program to encourage faculty to internationalize their teaching and research. The transplant also provided one hundred thousand dollars for a scholarship fund that would be administered by the university. Another university in the state received a grant from the United States–Japan Foundation for a three year project to expand and improve teaching about Japan and United States-Japan relations in K-12 classrooms throughout the Midwest. The project disseminated teaching resources, sponsored teacher workshops, conducted summer seminars, and provided minigrants to teachers to help them expand and improve their teaching on Japan (Becker, Wojtan, and Weathersby 1988).

Cultural programs in the community benefited from a grant from the State Humanities Council to fund a public lecture series on Japan for presentation to the general community. The transplant also participated in general community improvements by donating 111 cherry trees to county government for landscaping local parks and the county nursing home.

The business community promoted its interests in the transplant project by sponsoring a bus trip to a community in a contiguous state that was also the site of an auto transplant. Seventy people from government, media, schools, health services, and business met with their counterparts in the neighboring community to discuss a range of topics related to the transplant experience. Other activities of the business sector have focused on the establishment of a sister city project to facilitate a variety of exchanges with a city in Japan. Local business and political leaders have visited with counterparts in Japan under the general heading of cultural exchange, although the composition of delegations indicates they are focused on business ventures. Business contacts have been stimulated through by-invitation dinners with business and political leaders from Indiana and Japan, and through the activities of a university official who is responsible for maintaining university-autoplant relationships and facilitating joint business ventures in his role as a member of the state's Association of South East Asian Nations.

Segments of the religious community have been drawn into human relations projects that reflect their traditional concerns, but with a new emphasis. In the year before the transplant opened a representative of a local business group, the County Ministerial Association, and the local bishop cooperated to hire a consultant to come to the community and examine issues that might arise because of the transplant. After meeting with representatives from a variety of groups across the community the consultant developed a proposal for a "reconciliation project." The goals of the project included: "(a) Reconciliation of the people in different social/human segments of the community, (b) reconciliation of the people in the community and those who are represented by the automobile company." The consultant also recommended the creation of

> programs based on the maximum participation of all segments of the community. The major emphasis is on "ownership" by the participant. It is not sufficient that these programs be planned and implemented by the leadership of the community in isolation from the people of the community. (Buma Associates 1988:9)

In the year following the opening of the transplant the local ministerial association developed a human relations task force on topics of reconciliation, or bringing persons from different cultures together to enhance understanding. At around the same time, the business association involved with hiring the consultant contacted people from the local university who have worked for years with facilitating the integration of international students into the local community. This group formed an International Awareness Task Force as a part of the local Chamber of Commerce. The chamber provided space for task force meetings, staff to keep track of their proceedings, and eventually a grant application to a national philanthropic organization that is based in the state. A $19,600 grant was awarded to the chamber / task force to help workers, teachers, students, the business community, and others who deal with international residents to avoid misunderstanding or communicate more effectively with people of various cultures. A representative of the Chamber of Commerce said that "the grant money would be used to help develop training materials for local businesses to help their personnel deal with foreign customers." A local minister working on the task force recognizes its value but expresses some ambivalence:

> There is tension between trying to stay on the high moral ground which says all people have value and we can learn from them, and the more pragmatic approach that says internationals are customers and clients, so it's good for business. We must compromise to achieve a greater good, hopefully without compromising our principles. We have been working on improving intergroup understanding for twenty years, and I'm a little concerned to see how we are now focusing our work. We have to be sensitive to African-Americans and Hispanics who are saying "Why all the concern with the Japanese? We have been here for years."

The Indiana case represents an extensive and apparently successful effort to advance the process of embeddedness in the local community. There is, of course, nothing unusual about corporations wanting to be viewed as contributing members of the community. They typically do this through United Way contributions, support for the arts, and encouraging their management to participate in appropriate civic activities. What is noteworthy about the above-reported actions of the transplant, and its supporters from business, is the effort to reach into a variety of groups to create a favorable understanding of Japanese life, history, and culture through both people-to-people ties and organizational ties. One might even say that the ties that are established approach a level of institutional completeness, since they involve labor, business, polity, primary-secondary-postsecondary education, private foundations, religion, cultural associations, and civic organizations. When such ties can be put in the service of corporatist goals, we see the significance of embeddedness.

EMBEDDEDNESS IN KENTUCKY

The efforts to have the transplant project become embedded into the social groups that make up the community have been undertaken primarily by the Toyota Motor Corporation. Substantial financial contributions have been made by Toyota to a number of local and state programs:

1. Approximately $500,000 to local schools and charities.
2. $1 million to create a new community center in Georgetown.
3. An annual contribution of $200,000 to the Cardome Child Development Center.
4. $1 million to the University of Kentucky library.
5. $50,000 to Georgetown College.
6. $500,000 to Lexington's Thoroughbred Park.

In addition, Toyota has agreed to contribute $15 million over a twenty-year period to the Scott County School system. This was done because Toyota is exempt from paying property taxes under Industrial Revenue Bond Funding. Since school funds are based on property taxes Toyota agreed to make up for the school system's projected revenue loss.

These contributions by Toyota substantially exceed the monetary value of contributions by Subaru-Isuzu in Indiana. However, what is missing in Kentucky is evidence of embeddedness in a variety of grass roots community groups. The closest we get to people-to-people projects is Lexington's sister city relationship with Shinunai, the center of Japan's thoroughbred industry.

Persons interviewed in Scott County, Kentucky, were asked about civic, religious, cultural, or educational groups that had become involved with Japan, Japanese residents, or the transplant. The answers were as follows:

We don't have any programs with Japanese families. Transylvania College [in Lexington] has an ESL course [English as a Second Language] that is used by some of the wives.
The Saturday school for Japanese children is in Lexington, but we don't have anything in Georgetown.
I have heard that one of the local churches has services in Japanese, but I don't know the exact one.

The low level of involvement by the local community with projects related to Japan or the transplant may reflect the fact that Lexington is only fifteen miles from Georgetown. However, even the activities of the Japan society of Kentucky, which is located in Lexington, emphasizes business relationships rather than cultural or educational problems.

It is interesting that both Lafayette, Indiana, and Georgetown, Kentucky, are estimated to have about fifty to sixty Japanese families from the transplants living in their communities as long-term residents. Yet the communities differ quite dramatically on activities indicative of embeddedness. This may be due to the difference between the communities in the level of opposition to the transplants when the projects first started. Divisions in the business community in Kentucky, which emerged at the start of the project, may still be present at a level to discourage cooperative, cohesion-building efforts in the community.

EMBEDDEDNESS IN TENNESSEE

The Nissan Motor Corporation in Tennessee has made generous contributions to a number of local and state projects. It contributed $250,000 to health, civic, and cultural projects in the state, $35,000 for a new county ambulance, and $10,000 to a new $1 million recreational complex in Rutherford County. It has also contributed cherry trees to an art museum in Nashville; cosponsored, with Middle Tennessee State University and the Murfreesboro Little Theater, an Artists Residency program for Rutherford and surrounding counties; and cosponsored with the Japan Center of Tennessee an art and flower show at a city museum. Finally, it sponsored an automaker new car show in Nashville, a first in the area.

Independent of Nissan, the city of Hendersonville formed a sister city relationship with Tsuru, and hosted a visit of twenty-two officials and business people from Japan. Williams County's Association of Gifted started a Japanese language and culture program to enhance intercultural understanding.

It is interesting to note that Nissan made an effort to get involved in domestic politics that went awry. It sponsored a five-hundred-dollar-per-couple fund-raiser for a Tennessee congressman who had fought against "domestic content" legislation that would negatively affect transplants. Two senators from Tennessee and one congressman announced they would not attend the fund-raiser because of concern about a foreign firm getting involved in domestic politics.

The experience in Tennessee indicates somewhat more grass roots involvement in Japan-America projects than was found in Kentucky, but less than what was observed in Indiana. Overall, the findings on the amount of activity related to embeddedness in each state, and the success of those activities, are consistent with the predictions that were offered in Table 6.1.

EMBEDDEDNESS AND AFRICAN-AMERICANS

We offer one final speculation about the importance of embeddedness, and how it may have affected the opportunities for employment of African-Americans. A number of analysts of the transplants have noted that they are located in rural areas, some distance from cities with large black populations. As noted in Table 1.1, only Mazda in Michigan is located in a county with a substantial nonwhite population, thereby limiting the chances for employing African-Americans. A study of the site location and hiring practices at the transplants (Cole and Deskins 1988) indicates that several transplants have a work force that contains lower than the proportion of blacks in the labor pool in their areas. Thus, a combination of site location and hiring practices operates against hiring African-Americans in proportion to their representation in national and local populations.

Some analysts of Japanese business practices have suggested that what the Japanese do abroad is consistent with what they do at home. March (1993), an Australian business consultant who has worked in Japan, points out that the Japanese are very discriminatory in their hiring practices toward women, non–Japanese born (particularly Koreans), and those without the proper social and educational background.

How can these decisions by the transplants be related to embeddedness? One of the purposes of embeddedness is to achieve social and cultural integration of the transplant project and its Japanese families into the institutional fabric of the host community. This may be important because it makes good business sense, or because the Japanese place great importance on "being wanted" (Glickman and Woodward 1989:232). Whatever the reason, it is clear that those business and political leaders who pushed for the transplant also think embeddedness is important. Moreover, as we learned in Chapter 5, there is also an effort to capture the hearts and minds of workers by trying to create a common purpose between worker, company, and community.

It is therefore conceivable that this commitment to images of harmony, community, corporate family, and cultural integration could have led transplant decision-makers to avoid introducing potentially disruptive elements into their work force. The stereotypic and prejudiced views of high level Japanese officials are no secret. A former Japanese prime minister made disparaging remarks about African-Americans and other minorities in connection with the alleged decline in academic performance in the United States. A highly placed Japanese political leader was also cited for his gratuitous comments about the economic behavior of blacks. Without alleging prejudice or racism on the part of Japanese transplant executives, it can be assumed that they recognize that racial differences in the United States are a serious and potentially divisive social problem. They might, therefore, feel that it was wise to avoid hiring African-Americans because they would not be fully accepted by white co-workers or by the predominantly white communities where the plants are located.

Thus, the ideology of corporatism, and its implementation through social and cultural integration of the new corporate citizen, may have had the unanticipated result of producing a homogeneous work force that excluded nonwhites.

FINAL COMMENTS

In this chapter we have examined how transplants in Indiana, Kentucky, and Tennessee, once in place, attempt to become more fully integrated in the social and cultural system of their communities. We have described the process of becoming integrated as embeddedness, or the way that the structure and ideology of corporatism—the new partnership between business, government, and community—enter into a variety of social groups in the community.

Strongest support for the project comes from the business community. In contrast, environmental groups and labor are less supportive but they feel somewhat powerless to oppose the dominant coalition of the transplant, local politicians, and the business sector.

We have found support for our hypothesis that the effectiveness of the process of embeddedness is related to three characteristics of a community: (1) the interest of top management, (2) the extent of unity among the business class, and (3) the strength of organized opposition to the transplant at its initial conception. The transplant project becomes more fully integrated into a community when the transplant's top management is concerned about integration, when the business class is unified behind the project, and when organized opposition is weak.

Chapter 7

Capital and Community in Transition: Continuing Corporate Welfare or Nascent Social Economy?

The preceding chapters examined how the changing global economy led to the location of Japanese auto transplants in six states in the Midwest corridor and how the transplants, in turn, have shaped the social, political, and economic structures of the communities in which they located. Beginning in the mid-1960s and continuing through the 1970s, the U.S. economy experienced growing competition from other industrial nations and sagging profits from the domestic economy. The flight of capital out of the U.S. economy and the failure of U.S. business to invest in new plants and technology led to numerous plant closures and restructurings, and a loss of millions of high-wage jobs in manufacturing industries. One result of these economic changes was a decline in the strength of labor unions. Organized labor was unable to prevent the massive job loss or the flight of U.S. corporations and capital overseas. It was also unable to stem the loss of wages and benefits, and changing work rules that gave corporations greater control over day-to-day operations. A second result of the changing global and U.S. economy was declining revenue to state and local governments, which were coping with depressed local economies and reduced federal support for a variety of social programs and community infrastructure.

The U.S. auto industry, as one of the mainstays of the manufacturing sector, felt the full weight of the changing global economy. The success of foreign automakers in penetrating the U.S. market and challenging the once dominant Big Three resulted in severe cutbacks and streamlining at General Motors, Ford, and Chrysler. Employment at the Big Three, over one million workers in 1980, was heading toward a little over five hundred thousand by the mid-1990s. In 1990, one in every three cars sold in the United States was made by a foreign auto firm.

One of the more significant and far-reaching consequences of the changes described above was the emergence of the local state as entrepreneur. Although states have a long history of involvement in stimulating economic development, they would now fashion a new level of activism and a new set of strategies that would be qualitatively different from the past. We have referred to this emerging form of state activity as *corporatism*, an activist local state working with the business class to develop an industrial policy suited to the changing global economy. Corporatism spans the boundaries between public and private, capital and community, to create a belief in a new partnership of business, labor, and government working together for the common purpose of economic well-being for the state and local communities.

Coincident with the emergence of the local state as an activist partner in economic growth was the growing pressure on the Japanese auto industry to locate production facilities in the United States. Facing the threat of quotas on imports into the United States, Japanese companies began a search for suitable sites for the production of their cars and trucks in the United States. The result was an unprecedented interstate competition for the new auto assembly plants. Millions of dollars of public funds would be provided by states to foreign corporations as an incentive for the new plants.

Selling the idea of the corporatist project to different interest groups and the public required special efforts. The state as entrepreneur doling out millions in public money to outsiders was a somewhat novel concept. It was different from just providing tax abatements to get a new company or to help an existing company expand. State incentive packages involved putting money up front, and not simply forgoing tax revenue in the future. In order for the corporatist project to work it would have to be embraced by the community, which we referred to as the *process of embeddedness*.

We have tried to understand and assess the impact of the transplants on states and local communities through the theoretical lens of *embedded corporatism*. This has allowed us to bring together a number of disparate and independent actions by Japanese corporations, state political officials, local business elites, newspapers, and community groups into a coherent pattern of relationships that are changing the way that capital and community relate to each other. Some of these changes suggest a continuation and strengthening of the dominance of capital as it aligns itself with the state political regime and local business. The dominance of capital is expressed through a community's institutional leadership, which sanctions economic growth as the overriding meaning and purpose of collective community action. But there are also some changes that suggest the possibility of new capital-community relationships, and a conception of

community that permits nonmarket measures of community development. This can be seen in the small pockets of criticism of the corporatist
project that are designed to ensure that the transplant's actions are those
of a corporate citizen, which though large and powerful, is but one among
equals in the community.

Let us now try to elaborate on some of the contradictory tendencies
contained in changes brought forth by the transplants. In the next section
we look at the corporatist project as an example of business as usual, i.e.,
corporate dominance of the local community.

CORPORATE WELFARE AND CAPITAL-COMMUNITY TENSION

The most compelling conclusion to be drawn from our examination of
transplants in six midwestern states might be summed up with Calvin
Coolidge's phrase, "The business of America is business." The same coalition of corporate and political forces that were responsible for failures in
the auto and steel industries in the 1970s now stepped forward to take
advantage of new opportunities for profits. The actors may have changed,
but the objectives are the same. American corporations, facing a challenge
to large profits, did not think twice about closing plants, downsizing, or
investing abroad. The communities in which these decisions were played
out were only locations, not communities of people and institutions that
sustained plants during the good years.

Following deindustrialization, many corporations (both foreign and
American) saw new opportunities for capital investment as recession-
driven states competed for the promise of new jobs. Once again, it is the
wishes and needs of corporate capital that will dominate discussions with
states eager to have new corporate citizens.

Our study of Japanese transplants has yielded four large findings that
suggest that the corporatist project embodied in the transplant is but
another of a long record of private corporations using their control over
jobs as the tool to obtain political support and taxpayer's money.

Site Selection and Corporate Dominance

Available evidence on why the Japanese auto firms chose the states
they did to locate transplants indicates a shift away from purely economic
or organizational factors. Among the traditionally important location factors, only the existence of auto supplier firms continues to be an impor-

tant determinant of site selection. Transplants were located in states that already had a base of firms involved in the auto industry. In addition, location choice was also related to a number of factors associated with a state's administrative and political structure. States that attracted transplants had already made major commitments to pursue foreign investments, as evidenced by their administrative capacity and the allocation of resources to carry out recruitment of foreign firms.

The very substantial incentive packages provided by states to the transplants may have been at least as important for their political significance as for their economic value. The ability of a governor and a mayor to mobilize support for an incentive package provided evidence that political resources will be put in the service of business objectives. The incentive packages were the best evidence that could be provided of a strong partnership between government and business.

Thus, the selection of individual states as locations for transplants was based in an important way on the existence of a strong probusiness political system. It is the activist local state that is pushing the new corporatist partnership. And when this partnership is projected to include a six-state region containing successful corporatist projects, there is the potential for a model of local growth that will continue to dominate the agenda for state and regional economic development. Some analysts see the combination of transplants and a "lean and mean" Big Three as providing a brighter future for the Midwest. The Motor Vehicle Manufacturers Association estimates that the Midwest has 3 million jobs that are linked to motor vehicle production (*Chicago Fed Letter* 1993).

The success of the Midwest region in attracting transplants, expanding employment, and invigorating local economies does not mean that this can necessarily be reproduced elsewhere. Reindustrialization in the Midwest corridor is made possible by the flexibility with which capital and technology can be combined to revive mass production manufacturing in one region, small high-tech firms in another region, and low-wage sweatshops in another region. But this flexibility is dangerous in a volatile market environment. The structural changes in the location of manufacturing that hit the region in the 1980s could happen again, affecting both foreign and domestic auto firms. That is the nature of the changing global economy and how it interacts with the attributes of territorial area to create new opportunities for capital accumulation.

Boosterism and Corporatism

In the mid-1800s, cities in the Middle West were struggling to recover from a period of depression and financial crises that limited the availability of credit to farmers and merchants. The expansion of railroad networks and migration created new conditions for economic growth. Carl Abbott (1981) has written of this period by examining patterns of urban growth in four midwestern cities, and by examining the ideas of business and civic leaders who attempted to shape economic growth in their cities and region. The actions of this group of businessmen, politicians, "professional publicists" (i.e., newspapermen, magazine editors), clergymen, real estate developers, physicians, and attorneys to promote growth came to be known as *boosterism.*

These nineteenth-century boosters bear a strong resemblance to the modern-day proponents of growth who actively supported the corporatist projects in their communities. Yet despite the similarities in the political and business leaders who are the boosters and in their support for growth, there are several differences between nineteenth- and twentieth-century boosterism that are important to note.

The first difference is that the nineteenth-century boosters saw growth as serving a high purpose. Abbott provides evidence of how boosterism was linked to "national destiny"; "the United States. . .fit into world history"; "national purpose"; and "propitious social advancement" (1981: Chapter 9). Urban and regional boosterism promised the image of new cities, new ways of life, new philosophies, and new Americans who are "confident, assertive, hustling, and materialistic, they all believed in the rapid exploitation of the continent as a national duty" (p. 207).

The local boosters of today rarely get beyond discussing the opportunities for growth in a particular city, or perhaps a state. The vision is spatially anchored, and does not promise to reinvigorate a people or provide a new vision of the future. As a result, the modest hopes of local business and political leaders who are today's boosters and their calls to support a particular growth project are easily saddled with the suspicion of narrow self-interest. The state and local supporters of the transplant projects have tried to fashion a compelling vision that links particular growth projects to the aspirations of the larger community, but they have not done it in an open and forthright manner. Instead, today's boosters try to control the agenda of discussion about incentive packages or transplants, hoping to avoid any public opposition or input.

The second difference between nineteenth-century boosters and today's corporatist boosters is that in the former case growth was more firmly anchored in the small-business community. As Abbott stated in discussing the case of Indianapolis: "The city's growth came not from a few spectacular enterprises but from the measured operations of numerous small businesses" (1981:178). This point is underscored by contemporary scholars examining alternative approaches to growth who have argued that "a locally owned, independent restaurant can do more for a community than a McDonald's" (Gunn and Gunn 1991:132). This is also the position taken by critics of incentive packages for giant corporations, who argue instead for the use of incentives to support local businesses that may need help to expand their operations or to cope with a downturn in sales. Such efforts directed toward small businesses may ultimately provide the same employment base for a community at less cost, and with greater long-term contributions to the community's social fabric.

The conclusion to be drawn from this discussion is that although there is strong local involvement in each of the transplant projects, those who are involved represent a narrow segment of political and business groups. Moreover, their efforts do not resolve the tension between capital and community, but only manage it. The opposition to the transplant project that came from the small-business community in Kentucky, or the Farm Bureau in Tennessee appeared to be weak compared to the voices of support. However, this may tell us more about who dominates the local Chambers of Commerce today, and about local newspaper's coverage of the transplants, than about the strength of the opposition.

Cultural Integration of Corporatism

The corporatist project of bringing transplants to six communities in the Midwest corridor was much more than an economic endeavor. Years after the states' incentive packages were offered and accepted, and years after any public controversy about the incentives or the transplant had died down, supporters of the transplant would work slowly and deliberately to have the name of the transplant and the idea of a company-community partnership become an integral part of the community's cultural system.

The idea driving efforts directed toward cultural integration was always framed as a human relations issue. Reaching out to new people in a community has always been a part of middle-class life in small-town America. Often tied to the churches or activities involving new families in a school district, new people are welcomed to become part of the community. In the case of the transplant project, reaching out meant extending a welcome to people from a different language and culture.

In addition to the human relations motivation behind cultural integration was a second-level force: It was the decent thing to do and it was also good business. Executives of the transplants understood that being accepted by the community would ultimately help to create good labor-management relations. They also understood that it would help to create a feeling that the town and the plant were mutually involved in an endeavor that was vitally important to everyone. The local business and political leaders who were the main supporters of the transplant project also understood that there was latent suspicion of the idea of giving millions in tax dollars to a private corporation, and a foreign one no less. Not only a foreign firm, but a former enemy in World War II and our major competitor in the global economy.

The local business and political leaders believed that if the community embraced the transplant project it would also support future projects requiring the use of state and local tax dollars for large development projects. Thus, cultural integration of the transplants, or the process of embeddedness as we called it earlier, was an essential part of strengthening the belief in public-private joint projects as the new way of achieving economic growth. Corporatism, as a new way of thinking about relations between the public sector and the private sector, achieves its dominance as an ideology when it is embraced by broad segments of the community.

As noted in this research, the embeddedness process is not always fully successful. In some communities the efforts toward cultural integration are not embraced with enthusiasm. Some efforts have the appearance of being urged from the top down, rather than being created by local groups without economic interests in the transplant. As a result, efforts toward cultural integration will always have an element of tension between capital and community.

Labor and the Corporatist Project: Down But Not Out

At an early stage in this research project I was able to have a meeting with the CEO of one of the transplants. The meeting was arranged by a university official who was involved in some of the negotiations on the incentive package. The purpose of the meeting was to allow me to make a proposal to the CEO for a research project that I wanted to conduct. Prior to the meeting I prepared and submitted a written proposal of my project.

The meeting was held in a conference room and was attended by me, the university official, the Japanese CEO, a Japanese vice-president, and an American vice-president. Two Japanese secretaries were also present and took extensive notes during the meeting. After polite introductions and exchange of business cards, I was asked to make my presentation. I spoke for about twenty minutes, outlining a two-part project that involved first studying the transplant's training program for American team leaders that would be conducted in Japan during a three-month period, and second a survey of American production workers (associates) concerning their response to team leaders after start-up of production.

There were no questions during my presentation. When I finished, I thanked everyone for their attention and for the opportunity to present my proposal. All attention turned to the CEO who sat opposite me. He spoke: "Thank you for your interesting proposal. Now tell me, how do you feel about labor unions?"

This vignette is a good representation of the role played by labor in the corporatist project. Labor is rarely an official partner in the project or an active player, or even an agenda item in most discussions about the transplant. Yet the potential of labor always seems to be a latent concern. Labor often achieves standing as an actor of consequence because the transplants adopt policies or programs to limit labor's opportunity to organize. For example, a large component of the transplants' recruitment, selection, and training practices were concerned with getting workers with the right attitudes rather than the right skills. Similarly, efforts to resist or undercut unionizing efforts in transplants indicate that considerable resources are committed to deal with a nonplayer in the corporatist project.

The point of this discussion is that despite the extremely weak position of labor in the transplant communities and in the transplants themselves, they still receive a great deal of attention from management. Labor-management relations continue to be tense despite all the talk of cooperation, teamwork, and participation. The clear objective of management is to keep unions out of the transplants.

The role of organized labor in the transplants will be determined by two factors: job security and external labor markets. As long as the transplants do not violate the tacit commitment to a no-layoff policy, and as long as alternative jobs at higher wages are nonexistent, national labor unions will have a difficult time trying to organize in the transplants.

POSSIBILITIES FOR NEW CAPITAL-COMMUNITY ACCORDS

The previous section indicates the existence of continuing tension between the transplants and the communities in which they reside. The tension exists despite the dominance of the corporatist project, which is expressed through (1) the business-government partnership, (2) the support of local business in defining growth as synonymous with community, (3) cultural integration, and (4) the subordination of labor in the corporatist partnership.

The tensions in the corporatist project can be traced to divisions in the business class—especially small business—over the "special attention" that is given to foreign investors. The director of an economic development group in one transplant community identifies the difficulty he faced when attracting foreign investors:

The program that I developed to work with foreign investors was so successful that I started to get some grumbling from the "round eyes" who have been here for years. They sort of said, "What about us. How about a little publicity about what we do and what we need?"

There may also be divisions between the interests of international capital seeking sites for branch plants, and the local, property-oriented elite. Molotch and Logan (1984) discuss the sources of resistance to economic growth stimulated by international capital, and new strategies developed by capital to penetrate local communities.

Another source of tension in the corporatist project is related to a general suspicion among the general public about the idea of giving money to large corporations. The public seems to be ambivalent about the new partnership, recognizing the economic benefits but reluctant to fully embrace the practice of incentive packages for business. The community surveys conducted by Houghland (1993) provide clear evidence of this ambivalence. Annual surveys of Scott County, Kentucky, residents between 1986 and 1990 indicate that between 51 and 56 percent of those surveyed believe that the "Toyota plant will benefit the people of Kentucky enough to justify the expense." At the same time, they also express less agreement with the statement "I support the idea of state funding for the Toyota plant in Scott County." In 1986 there was 45 percent agreement with the statement, and it declined to 37 percent in 1990.

I believe that these tensions can be added to those that exist among transplant workers who, although pleased to have good-paying, reasonably secure jobs, are very aware of the workplace demands that they face each day on the line. The tensions in the corporatist project provide a basis for changes in the way that transplants relate to their host communities and their workers.

I would like to close this book by pointing to some of the small possibilities for changing the relationship between corporations, workers, and the communities in which they reside. I am assuming, first of all, that the success to date of the corporatist project represented by the transplants will encourage many similar efforts by foreign and domestic corporations. Many other communities like Flat Rock, Bloomington/Normal, Marysville, Lafayette, Georgetown, and Smyrna will be asked to put up public money to attract a new corporate citizen. What hope is there for other communities to have corporate citizens without being subservient to them? What are the chances that communities can put forward and defend qualitative measures of their well-being? What are the prospects for corporate citizens to act like "persons" in their commitments to the workers and communities that sustain them? These questions are about moving beyond corporation-community tensions to corporation-community accords.

Community Control of Corporations

Most efforts to control or limit the negative impacts of corporations have been via regulatory and legal means. The Environmental Protection Agency looks out for the neighbors of corporations who might be harmed by air and water emissions. The Occupational Health and Safety Administration seeks to eliminate unsafe conditions in the workplace that are responsible for worker injuries and deaths. The Food and Drug Administration tries to inform customers about the quality of their food and the safety of their medicines.

The limited effectiveness of legislative and regulatory means to limit the harm done by corporations is well-known. Let us take the case of plant-closing legislation, which is related to the concerns of this book. In 1988, in the heat of a presidential campaign between George Bush and Michael Dukakis, Congress passed the Worker Assistance and Retraining Notification Act (WARN). WARN was a plant-closing bill requiring companies to provide a sixty-day notice of shutdowns and layoffs to their employees. Although outgoing President Reagan was opposed to the bill, he was persuaded by congressional Republicans not to veto it because they feared that strong public support for the bill could hurt the Republicans in the election.

The plant-closing law that was passed was very modest compared to some of the proposed legislation which had called for six-month notification, severance pay, one year of health insurance, job transfer privileges, funds for worker retraining, and payments to the community (Perrucci et al. 1988). However, even the modest law that was passed (prescribing only a sixty-day notice of a closing) has been still weaker in its administration. First of all, the law has a large loophole that exempts companies that claim lack of sufficient advanced knowledge of their financial situation or that claim that early disclosure of closing plans would harm their business operations by loss of financing, cooperation from suppliers, or unfair competition. Second, there is no government monitoring or enforcement mechanism to see that companies give a sixty-day notice. The Department of Labor does not enforce the law, but waits for displaced workers or their unions to bring suits against companies that fail to provide advance warning.

The point of this discussion is that the legislative approach to control or limit the actions of corporations is usually very weak, and enforcement often gets bogged down in years of litigation in federal courts. Workers or communities that are harmed by plant closings often lack the resources to engage in prolonged legal proceedings. So why not link such policies as plant-closing legislation to the packages of incentives that communities provide to many corporations? In the case of the transplants, a state's incentive package, which provides tens of millions in inducements for an auto firm to choose its site, could also specify obligations on the part of the transplant to employ a certain number of workers, to stay open for a specified period of time, to provide paybacks to the community if it should decide to leave or substantially reduce production. This would result in a more symmetrical relationship between the community and the transplant, with each party receiving benefits and incurring obligations. Such arrangements would also give substance to the belief that transplants provide their workers with job security, and thereby promise the community long-term commitments to its economic base.

There is evidence from a number of the communities studied in this book that transplants are sensitive to the concerns and criticisms of the host community. In Georgetown, Kentucky, the Toyota plant holds regular meetings with persons from local environmental groups. It also meets with a Chamber of Commerce–sponsored group to discuss a variety of concerns, including child care facilities at the transplant. Such relationships could move beyond mere public relations efforts to establish a community's right to deal with matters of environment or child care or traffic congestion. A corporate-community board could be created to discuss such topics, or community representatives could be appointed to the board of directors of the transplant.

Concern over the corporate-community relationship is reflected in an ongoing legal battle over the right of General Motors to close one of its auto assembly plants. In February 1993, a Michigan judge issued a ruling that prevented GM from closing its Willow Run assembly plant in Ypsilanti, Michigan. The judge's ruling concluded that GM gave assurances to Ypsilanti that it would be able to continue production in return for $13 million in tax abatements. In August 1993, a three-justice appeals court reversed the earlier ruling, arguing that GM did not make promises, but "expressions of [its] hopes or expectations of continued employment at Willow Run." An attorney for the Township of Ypsilanti has indicated that the appeals court ruling would be brought to the Michigan Supreme Court.

Regardless of the particular means used, greater community control can be exercised over the transplants, and it may be more effective in achieving certain goals than what is provided by federal and state regulatory agencies. As communities become more involved in providing for the financial, cultural, and social needs of transplants, they can be expected to have greater opportunities to influence corporate decisions.

Workplace Democracy

We have noted the high value placed on human resources in the transplants. Much is made of the role of workers as among the most valued
assets that any company can have. Two aspects of Japanese management
principles applied to the social organization of work are very important, if
they are taken seriously. First, is the idea of continuous improvement of
the work process, with workers playing a key role in that process. This
idea views workers as continuously learning and taking on new skills. It
is contrary to a machine-centered perspective, which emphasizes highly
specialized, deskilled labor that can be replaced with ease. The second
idea involves cooperative work teams, which shifts attention away from
the isolated skills of a single worker to the collective skills of a work
group.

Taken together, these two ideas have the *potential* for giving workers
greater control over the work process, and for building bonds of solidarity among workers. Whether that potential can be converted into actual worker control over important decisions seems remote at the present
time. But given present conditions of weak labor organization and the
continuing threat of job loss, work team structures and expanded skills
may be the only collective source of strength available to workers in
transplants. The dilemma facing labor today is recognized by labor advocates who seem to be saying that participation, cooperation, and teamwork is the only game in town (Bluestone and Bluestone 1992). However,
there are powerful arguments against participation and teamwork, view-
ing them simply as new management strategies to extract profits and
undercut unionization (Fantasia, Clawson, and Graham 1988).

While I am not particularly optimistic about the likelihood that greater
workplace democracy will develop from skill expansion and work teams,
if such forms of work organization are combined with attempts at community control of the transplants, as discussed in the previous section,
then it is possible that something new and important may be developing.
It is also possible to think of bonds of solidarity developing among
workers beyond the boundaries of a single plant. Each of the transplants
is in close proximity to dozens of supplier firms, creating a spatial concentration of thousands of workers, their families, and friends. Schwartz
and Romo (1992) have noted how the concentration of assembly plants
and suppliers increases chances for the recognition of common interests and the possibilities for coordinated actions. At the very least, workers might become involved in conventional local politics as a way to
advance their interests. This view of the potential political significance of
a spatially concentrated work force is reminiscent of Marx's hypothesis
that the concentration of urban industrial workers in close proximity to

the factories would contribute to the emergence of class consciousness and a politically active working-class movement (see, e.g., Bendix and Lipset 1966).

A Regional Social Economy

The final possibility for significant change in corporate-community relations is in creating a regional focus for economic restructuring. This is an intermediate form of restructuring that lies between the ambitious call for a national industrial policy orchestrated from Washington, D.C., and the competitive spatially anchored efforts to spur growth in a particular city or state. It is also an effort to bridge the economy-community gap by referring to a social economy rather than a *market* economy. A social economy looks at a community as a place to work and live, and thereby attempts to balance the requirements of economic growth with the requirements of the total community for clean air and water, good schools, supportive social services, and affordable homes. A social economy is concerned with developing human resources that can serve the needs of a region and not simply a particular company.

Severyn Bruyn (1977, 1991) has argued persuasively for the development and application of a social economy, one that moves beyond the narrow self-interest and rational choice of neoclassical economics, and the emphasis on the role of power in shaping economic life that is central to political economy. The concept of social economy is broader and more inclusive than alternative approaches, stressing the full array of institutional linkages between economy and society. If neoclassical economics is "disembedded" from society (Bruyn 1991:27), a social economy is concerned with the totality of social forces, market and nonmarket exchange relationships, and societal normative systems that do not simply *impinge on* economic activities, but *constitute* economic activities.

Consideration of a social economy introduces questions of purpose and value when assessing economic activity. It makes a difference whether a factory makes bombs or bicycles. It makes a difference if land development and growth bring jobs but make a community a less desirable place to live. It makes a difference if the jobs created by growth do not provide security or opportunities to use and develop new skills. A social economy is an *organic economy* that includes a community's social, political, and economic institutions. It emphasizes interdependence, cooperation, and community-centered values while trying to balance the needs of people as producers and consumers. A social economy directly confronts the abuses of capitalism by emphasizing democratic principles in decision-making and putting the needs of people and community before profits.

Bruyn (1991:321) sees the opportunities for thinking about a social economy reflected in recent changes such as employee ownership, greater worker participation in management, the growth of nonprofit organizations, and trade associations that allow for competition and self-regulation. Block (1990) sees similar opportunities to emphasize "qualitative growth" as an alternative way of organizing an economy. Growth that would produce efficiency while providing greater democracy in the form of "cooperative arrangements between employees and employers that sustain employees' motivation, encourage them to be heard, and assure high levels of investment in the development of their skills" (p. 199).

I believe that the corporatist project embodied in the transplants provides a similar opportunity to think about a social economy, but at a more modest, regional level. The corporatist project has, in an unintended way, started a process of "reembedding" capitalism within the social institutions of the community. In the process of getting the project embraced by the community, some of its advocates spoke not simply of economic benefits, but of the promise to preserve "a way of life," "the Bluegrass community," or "the virtues of small-town America." If this promise is taken seriously by the community, and used as an evaluative standard for the corporatist project, it may be possible to combine economic and community standards and needs when discussing development and growth.

Building a regional social economy is no simple matter. Markusen (1987) has examined the politics and economics of regions and has identified from historical research some of the elements of successful regional organizing. First, and perhaps foremost, a region must have an economic base that is strong enough to unify the interests of the several states and to sustain a wide array of economic activities. An automobile production complex has the potential for providing such an economic base because of the size of its employment base, its relatively high wage structure, and its contribution to secondary employment and business activity. Second, there must be limited intraclass and interclass antagonism. The business and working classes must be internally unified to support regionalism, and they must believe that they will both benefit from the effort to build a regional social economy. The business class may see the benefits of a stable economy that avoids the risks of the boom and bust business cycle. For the working class there is the promise of more secure employment; and when unemployment occurs there are extensive programs for retraining and reentry into the labor market. Third, the elected senators and representatives from a region must make place-based politics part of the national agenda by acting in concert to foster legislation that supports their region. The six-state region in the Midwest corridor has twelve senators and eighty-one representatives in the U.S. Congress. Their actions, and those of state governments, can increase the chances for an industrial policy that would support the U.S. auto industry in the face of global competition. Their actions could produce regionally based aid programs for cities, displaced workers, retraining, housing, education, and transportation.

Several developments discussed in this book argue for consideration of a regional social economy. First, the changing global economy is characterized by great flexibility. We will see the simultaneous development of mass-production manufacturing and small firms using highly skilled workers to create and develop new products. We will also see the reappearance of sweatshop firms that exploit the availability of vulnerable populations of immigrants in highly competitive markets such as clothing and textiles. Unless there is a national policy to limit the freedom of capital to invest where and how it wishes, it will be difficult to fashion an industrial policy that can deal with such a diverse economy. Similarly, it will be difficult for a state (and certainly a community) to find an adaptation to the global economy that provides some measure of security about the future. But a multistate region may have the resources and flexibility needed to adapt to a changing global economy. And a multistate region may also have greater capacity to exercise broad social control over the investment process.

The second development that argues for the idea of a regional social economy is the need for a work force capable of what Sabel (1993:139) calls "permanent innovation," and the inability of organized labor, or federal retraining programs to provide workers who are continually involved in retraining. Some of this type of retraining is done in specific firms, but the focus is on the skills needed in that firm at that time, and not on the broader regional economy. There must be social responsibility for retraining workers and developing the human resources needed to compete in the global economy. Communities, states, corporations, and labor must work together to develop continuous training programs for workers. This can serve the needs of displaced workers and stimulate the kind of shop floor innovation that is needed to compete in a global economy.

A regional social economy would be based on genuine collaborative arrangements between workers, unions, communities, governments, and business that could stimulate growth, retrain workers, foster worker self-management, and involve communities in participatory and democratic decision-making. Thinking about a regional social economy will require (1) community-corporation agreements that move beyond incentive packages to shared responsibility for economic and social development, (2) new intrafirm workplace organization that stresses worker participation in key decisions bearing on productivity and job security, and (3) new

interfirm agreements that encourage cooperative research and development and worker retraining.

There are examples of interfirm and interstate cooperation, but they are
not directed at trying to develop a regional social economy. Auto supplier
firms that work with Toyota are expected to join the Bluegrass Automotive Manufacturers Association, which was started by Toyota in 1990
(Kenney and Florida 1993). The objective of this association is to get
suppliers to share information and cooperate in ways that contribute to
productivity and quality. Bruyn (1991) examines the role of trade associations in several U.S. sectors of the economy that have the potential to
regulate interfirm competition and advance the public interest. Such associations can be strengthened by government action to encourage their role
in self-regulation.

At the level of state governments, Seeman (1992) has pointed to the
existence of the U.S./Japan Southeast Association, composed of seven
states and represented by their governors, as examples of the possibility
of regional corporatism. This association meets annually, alternating
among states and meeting in Japan every other year. Each governor is
accompanied by a state delegation of elected officials (e.g., mayors), economic development directors, economists, and private-sector executives.
One participant in the association describes the annual meetings as occa-
sions for states to advertise what they are doing to foster economic development and what they can offer firms looking for location sites. The
agenda for these meetings seems to be more competitive than cooperative, as evidenced by the report that Kentucky was turned down when it
sought to join the seven member states in the association.

The potential for a regional social economy depends upon whether the
transplant project in the six-state region is developed into a genuine core
industry. We know that the assembly plants in the six states have attracted a large number of smaller parts suppliers to the region. The supplier firms operate in a very competitive environment, and their wage
structures and working conditions do not compare favorably to those in
the assembly plants. At present, the assembly plants do not provide the
full range of research, design, and development inputs that would reflect
a fully developed core industry. Moreover, some of the most important
components of the finished auto, such as the engine and transmission, are
produced outside the country and imported by the transplants. These
components are produced by a more highly skilled work force than is
found in the assembly plants, and their work contributes greater value to
the final product.

There is considerable disagreement about whether the transplants will
form the basis for a fully developed automotive industry in the Midwest
corridor. Kenney and Florida (1993) believe that the transplants are not

simply "screwdriver" plants, using low-skilled workers to assemble parts that are produced elsewhere. They point to the fact that the transplants have added research and development facilities in several locations in the United States, including Kentucky, Ohio, and Michigan. These new facilities are involved in product design and engineering work, and the intent of transplants is to produce cars in the United States from design to final assembly. Florida and Kenney believe that the supplier firms are also moving, albeit more slowly, to establish research and development units capable of developing an infrastructure that provides the innovations needed for a dynamic industry. As Florida and Kenney state:

> One can envision a scenario wherein Japanese corporations develop localized and semi-autonomous innovation-production centers that are responsible for design and production of cars for a specific regional market (e.g. Japan, United States, or Europe). These regional systems would then be linked together in a corporate hierarchy with Tokyo and its center. Some standardized and smaller parts would flow throughout the corporate network, but many would be produced locally. The most advanced R&D might be done in a central, typically Japanese facility; however, product development related to production would be carried out by the local complex. Of course, important innovations would diffuse internationally throughout the complex. (p. 154)

A much less optimistic view is provided by Howes (1993), who states that the Japanese do not intend to build a fully integrated automobile production system in the United States. Instead, U.S. transplants will function as branch plants, importing parts that are based on more advanced design and engineering skills and technology. Howes's argument starts with an examination of how Japan's national policy of emphasizing exports is linked to its production organization and industrial relations, which stress nonmarket incentives. The special relationships that Japanese firms develop with their domestic work force and suppliers have produced greater job security and long-term cooperative relations with suppliers. This has resulted in high levels of productivity and growth through exports. Thus, there is very little incentive to risk disrupting their production organization by shifting more facilities from Japan to the United States. Instead, they will transfer enough to give them access to the U.S. market and the advantages of lower cost labor.

Florida and Kenney have suggested that the productivity of the Japanese transplants is due to their success in transferring an integrated production system to the United States. Howes argues that productivity advantages in transplants are due to lower labor costs. Transplant workers are younger and have less costly health benefits and retirement programs (Howes 1991b). Moreover, their parts suppliers are low-wage, nonunion plants, providing another cost advantage over Big Three firms, whose suppliers are more likely to be unionized. Howes also suggests that the estimates of the domestic content of autos produced at the trans-plants is artificially inflated, and therefore do not support the belief that the transplants have established a concentrated network of domestic sup-pliers that provide a full range of parts through collaborative efforts. Howes's view is as follows:

> Complex, engineering-intensive and difficult to manufacture components such as engine, transmission, suspension, steering and electronic controls are the real heart of the vehicle. Their development must take place as the car itself is being designed. The earlier suppliers are involved in the design process, the lower the overall development and manufacturing costs and the shorter the lead time necessary for product development. For Japanese firms the typical lead time is 4 years compared to 8 years in U.S. firms. They are integral to the identity of a vehicle. These complex parts are generally delivered as part of a system. The supplier must coordinate other suppliers and be involved in the design process of the vehicle. Having the suppliers of parts or system components close by and intimately involved in the design process gives firms—Japanese firms—an enormous competitive advantage in terms of cost, lead time and quality. (These are the components which every emerging auto-producing country wants to build because they em-body the most sophisticated product and production technologies.) Mexico, for example, requires domestic production of engines and transmissions as a condition of sale in the local market.
>   That is why these components are not being built in-house by the trans-plant assemblers, nor sourced from outside suppliers in the United States. They are being designed and largely manufactured in Japan in collaborative relationships between the firms and the suppliers. The transplants are per-forming only assembly and stamping at their twelve assembly plants. (1993:19)

If Florida and Kenney are correct, the Midwest corridor will be the location of an integrated automobile production complex that will serve as a core industry for the region. Jobs will be available in the transplants as well as in more highly skilled engineering and design facilities and in supplier firms. Such a production complex would contribute to a wide range of business activity in financial and professional services that will be needed to sustain a state-of-the-art auto industry technology.

If Howes is correct, the Midwest corridor will be the location of a "hollowed-out" auto industry that assembles autos from parts produced elsewhere. Auto suppliers in the region will provide simple parts that require little engineering and unskilled workers. The region will not de-velop the economic strength of a core industry that is capable of stimulat-ing and sustaining long-term growth for communities throughout the region. Transplants will continue to be important for local economies, but as "screwdriver" plants they will remain vulnerable to a volatile environment that shifts the technology of manufacturing and the location of manufacturing activity. Without the economic power of an integrated auto production complex, transplants would have little choice but to reduce labor costs when faced with weak markets and excess inventory.

The full impact of the corporatist project on the Midwest corridor is uncertain. The investment of almost $1 billion of public money for direct and indirect support of the six transplants may turn out to have revitalized the region's economy and reestablished the auto industry as a core economy. Or it may turn out to be just another case of corporate welfare, with public money being provided to private firms who pursue opportunities without obligations to the communities in which they reside.

Appendix

A Note on Method

This book is about the transplant project, the location of Japanese auto assembly plants in six states in the Midwest corridor. I have tried to provide a composite account of why the Japanese chose to locate where they did, how states developed and presented the idea of using incentives to attract transplants, and what all this has meant for the workers and communities in which the transplants are located.

A political economy approach has been used to understand the transplant phenomenon. This means that the experiences and actions of local communities and states were studied in relation to the global economic and political forces that affect them. Moreover, the phenomenon under examination was placed in a historical context, so that the actions of communities in the 1980s were seen as grounded in past experiences and providing opportunities for future developments.

A political economy approach also led us to see the actions of corporations, political officials, workers, environmentalists, and business people involved in the transplant project as reflections of opposed interests of contending social groups and classes. Economic development policies and programs in a local community are shaped by the competing interests of social groups and classes.

The research for this book was carried out over a period of approximately four years. During the first two years, most of the research effort was spent reading available literature on local and state level economic development, on the U.S. automobile industry, and on foreign investment in the United States. Time devoted to the research project increased during the third year as the outlines of the overall project started to take shape. Systematic content analysis of several newspapers was carried out during this year, and interviews, face to face and telephone, were conducted with local and state economic development officials.

With the support of a fellowship from the Center for Research on the Social and Behavioral Sciences at Purdue University, and a sabbatical

167

leave, the author worked full-time on the project for a period of fifteen months. This involved reading and content analysis of six newspapers, site visits to Georgetown, Kentucky, and Smyrna, Tennessee, and personal interviews with a variety of persons (described below) in three states.

Information for this book was obtained from a variety of published sources, and they are documented throughout the text. Other data that were not available were obtained in the following manner.

DOCUMENTS

The official agreements between the six states and the six Japanese auto firms were obtained from state officials under available freedom of information guidelines.

Transplant firms provided documents about building plans, recruitment and training programs, and guiding managerial philosophies. These were primarily public relations materials that were designed for press releases or for organized plant tours.

National and state Japan-American Society offices provided material describing their membership, purposes, and annual activities. These were essentially "annual reports" available to interested parties.

NEWSPAPERS

A total of twelve years of daily newspaper issues were read and systematically analyzed. Two newspapers each from Indiana, Kentucky, and Tennessee were selected in order to study coverage of the auto transplant in the state. One newspaper was from the local community closest to the site of the transplant and one was a state newspaper. The two papers in Indiana were the *Lafayette Journal and Courier* and the *Indianapolis Star*. In Kentucky they were the *Lexington Herald-Leader*, and the *Louisville Courier-Journal*. In Tennessee, the newspapers were the *Murfreesboro Daily News Journal*, and the *Nashville Tennessean*.

The first year of newspaper coverage of the transplants in each of the six publications was systematically read to identify any item that was concerned with the transplant. Each item (news story, editorial, letter to the editor, paid advertisement) was analyzed as noted in Chapter 4. A second year of coverage of the transplants in the six papers was also read and analyzed. This involved the year in which the transplant was officially opened, and the coverage was for six months before and after the plant start-up date.

The author also read materials from the *Bloomington Journal Star* in Illinois, and the *Columbus Dispatch* in Ohio. These materials were not obtained in the same systematic fashion as the other newspapers. One year of the *Columbus Dispatch* was examined (the year of the new plant opening) but it was not systematically analyzed. Other newspaper items were sent to me by colleagues in Illinois and Ohio who knew of my research interest in the transplants.

INTERVIEWS

A total of fifty-two persons were interviewed, either by telephone or in person. With the exception of state-level economic development officials, almost all interviews were of persons involved in the transplant project in Indiana, Kentucky, and Tennessee. The numbers of persons interviewed from different sectors of the community are as follows:

6   CEOs, industrial firms, land development firms
4   mayors, former mayors
9   education and religious organizations
17 Departments of Commerce, Planning, and Human Resources
4   labor union officials
2   directors of environmental organizations
3   Chamber of Commerce officials
3   Japan American Society officials
4   executives and associates at transplants

CONSULTATION

During the course of this project the author attended profession-al/scholarly conferences and engaged in the exchange of information on matters related to the U.S. auto industry and the Japanese transplants. The author exchanged working papers with several colleagues as a way of testing a variety of preliminary ideas about the changing global economy and the significance of the auto transplants.

The most important perspective that is missing from this book is that of workers (associates) in the transplants. It is not possible to get lists of workers from the transplants, and in the absence of unions (at four of the six plants) it is not possible to try and reach workers through their unions. Instead, we have relied on the small number of studies that focus on workers (Fucini and Fucini 1990; Graham 1991) and on newspaper accounts. It is important to have better information on how workers in the transplants feel about their managers and the conditions under which they labor.

Information from all of the above sources has been combined to produce an ethnographic case study of Japanese auto transplants in six states. It is not an in-depth study of one transplant, but a composite picture of the transplant project as it developed in the six states. We have tried to identify and interpret the common experiences of six communities as well as some of their differences. I hope that the effort enables us to see the transplant-community relationship in a new way.

References

Abbott, Carl. 1981. *Boosters and Businessmen: Popular Economic Thought and Urban Growth in the Antebellum Middle West.* Westport, CT: Greenwood.

Aldrich, Howard E. and Jeffrey Pfeffer. 1976. "Environments of Organizations." In A. Inkeles (ed.), *Annual Review of Sociology* 2:79–106, Annual Reviews Inc.

Alexander, Lamar. 1986. *Friends: Japanese and Tennesseans.* Tokyo: Kodansha.

Alston, Jon P. 1989. *The American Samurai: Blending American and Japanese Managerial Practices.* Hawthorne, NY: Aldine de Gruyter.

Altschull, J. Herbert. 1984. *Agents of Power: The Role of the News Media in Human Affairs.* White Plains, NY: Longman.

Ashton, Patrick J. and Peter Iadicola. 1986. "The Differential Impact of a Plant Closing on the Re-employment and Income Patterns of Displaced Blue- and White-Collar Employees." Presented at the annual meeting of the North Central Sociological Association, Toledo, Ohio.

Bachelor, Lynn W. 1991. "Michigan, Mazda, and the Factory of the Future: Evaluating Economic Development Incentives." *Economic Development Quarterly* 5(May):114–25.

Bartik, Timothy J. 1991. *Who Benefits From State and Local Economic Development Policies.* Kalamazoo, MI: Upjohn Institute.

Becker, James, Linda Wojtan, and Kathryn Weathersby. 1988. "Midwest Program for Teaching about Japan: Final Report." National Clearinghouse for United States–Japan Studies, Indiana University, Bloomington.

Bendix, Reinhard and Seymour M. Lipset. 1966. "Karl Marx's Theory of Social Classes." Pp. 6–11 in *Class, States, and Power,* edited by R. Bendix and S. M. Lipset. New York: Free Press.

Berggren, Christian. 1992. *Alternatives to Lean Production.* Ithaca, NY: Industrial and Labor Relations Press.

Berggren, Christian, Torsten Bjorkman, and Ernest Hollander. 1991. *Are They Unbeatable? Report from a Field Trip to Study Transplants.* Stockholm: Royal Institute of Technology.

Blair, John P. and Robert Premus. 1987. "Major Factors in Industrial Location: A Review." *Economic Development Quarterly* 1:72–85.

Block, Fred. 1987. *Revising State Theory.* Philadelphia: Temple University Press.

———. 1990. *Postindustrial Possibilities.* Berkeley: University of California Press.

171

Bluestone, Barry and Bennett Harrison. 1982. *The Deindustrialization of America.* New York: Basic Books.

Bluestone, Irving and Barry Bluestone. 1992. *Negotiating the Future: A Labor Perspective on American Business.* New York: Basic Books.

Book of the States. Lexington, KY: Council of State Governments.

Bruyn, Severyn T. 1977. *The Social Economy: People Transforming Modern Business.* New York: Wiley.

————. 1991. *The Future of the American Economy: The Social Market.* Stanford, CA: Stanford University Press.

Buma Associates, Inc. 1988. *Report and Proposals to the Task Force on Reconciliation.* Lafayette, IN: Tippecanoe County Ministerial Association.

Castells, Manuel and Jeffrey Henderson. 1987. "Techno-economic Restructuring. Socio-Political Processes and Spatial Transformation: A Global Perspective." Pp. 1–17 in *Global Restructuring and Territorial Development,* edited by Jeffrey Henderson and Manuel Castells. Beverly Hills: Sage.

Cawson, Alan. 1985. "Varieties of Corporatism: The Importance of the Meso-level of Interest Intermediation." Pp. 1–21 in *Organized Interests and the State,* edited by Alan Cawson. Beverly Hills: Sage.

Census of Governments. 1982. Washington, DC: U.S. Department of Commerce, Bureau of the Census.

Chicago Fed Letter. 1993. "Auto Industry Restructuring and the Midwest Economy." *Federal Reserve Bank of Chicago* 70(June).

Cohen, Stephen and John Zysman. 1987. *Manufacturing Matters: The Myth of the Post-Industrial Economy.* Washington, DC: Office of Technology Assessment.

Cole, Robert E. and Donald Deskins, Jr. 1988. "Racial Factors in Site Location and Employment Patterns of Japanese Auto Firms in America." *California Management Review* (Fall):9–22.

Coleman, James S. 1990. *Foundations of Social Theory.* Cambridge, MA: Belknap Press of Harvard University Press.

Coleman, Vernon. 1988. "Labor Power and Social Equality: Union Politics in a Changing Economy." *Political Science Quarterly* 103:687–705.

Cornfield, Daniel. 1989. "The Japanese Challenge." *St. Petersburg Times,* August 6, p. 10.

County and City Data Book. 1985. Washington, DC: U.S. Government Printing Office.

Cowan, J. Tadlock and Frederick H. Buttel. 1988. "Subnational Corporatist Policymaking: The Organization of State and Regional High-Technology Development." Pp. 241–68 in *Research in Politics and Society, Vol. 3, Deindustrialization and the Restructuring of American Industry,* edited by M. Wallace and J. Rothschild. Greenwich, CT: JAI.

Cusumano, Michael. 1985. *The Japanese Automobile Industry.* Cambridge, MA: Harvard University Press.

Directory of Incentives to Business. 1986. National Association of State Development Agencies. Washington, DC: Urban Institute Press.

Dirks, Herman. 1992. "The Global Partnership." Presented at a conference on Global Partners: Local Communities and Japanese Transplants, Illinois Wesleyan University, October 22–24.

Drier, Peter. 1982. "The Position of the Press in the U.S. Power Structure." *Social Problems* 29:298–310.

Dye, Thomas R. 1985. *Politics in States and Communities.* Englewood Cliffs, NJ: Prentice-Hall.

Education Directory. Various years. National Center for Educational Statistics. Washington, DC: U.S. Department of Education.

Eisenger, Peter. 1988. *The Rise of the Entrepreneurial State.* Madison: University of Wisconsin Press.

Fantasia, Rick, Dan Clawson, and Gregory Graham. 1988. "A Critical View of Worker Participation in America." *Work and Occupations* 15(November):468–88.

Feagin, Joe R. and Michael Peter Smith. 1987. "Cities and the New International Division of Labor." Pp. 3–34 in *The Capitalist City: Global Restructuring and Community Politics,* edited by Michael P. Smith and Joe R. Feagin. New York: Basil Blackwell.

Ferman, Louis A. 1984. "The Political Economy of Human Services: The Michigan Case." *International Journal of Mental Health* 13:125–38.

Flaim, Paul O. and Ellen Sehgal. 1985. "Displaced Workers in 1979–83: How Well Have They Fared?" *Monthly Labor Review* 108:3–16.

Florida, Richard and Martin Kenney. 1991. "Transplanted Organizations: The Transfer of Japanese Industrial Organization to the U.S." *American Sociological Review* 56:381–98.

Florida, Richard, Martin Kenney, and Andrew Mair. 1988. "The Transplant Phenomenon: Japanese Auto Manufacturers in the United States." *Economic Development Commentary* 12(Winter 1988):3–9.

Fox, William F. 1990. "Japanese Investment in Tennessee: The Economic Effects of Nissan's Location in Smyrna." Pp. 175–87 in *The Politics of Industrial Recruitment,* edited by E. J. Yanarella and W. C. Green. New York: Greenwood.

Fucini, Joseph J. and Suzy Fucini. 1990. *Working for the Japanese: Inside Mazda's American Auto Plant.* New York: Free Press.

Fujita, Kuniko and Richard Child Hill. 1993. "Toyota's City: Industrial Organizations and the Local State in Japan." In *Japanese Cities in the World Economy,* edited by Kuniko Fujita and Richard Child Hill. Philadelphia: Temple University Press.

Gelsanliter, David. 1992. *Jump Start: Japan Comes to the Heartland.* New York: Kodansha International.

Glickman, Norman J. and Douglas P. Woodward. 1989. *The New Competitors: How Foreign Investors Are Changing the U.S. Economy.* New York: Basic Books.

Goodman, Robert. 1979. *The Last Entrepreneurs: America's Regional Wars for Jobs and Dollars.* New York: Simon and Schuster.

Gordon, David, Richard Edwards, and Michael Reich. 1982. *Segmented Work, Divided Workers.* Cambridge: Cambridge University Press.

Graham, Laurie. 1991. "Production Control: A Case Study of a Japanese Automobile Transplant." Presented at the annual meeting of the North Central Sociological Association in Dearborn, Michigan, April 25–28.

Granovetter, Mark. 1985. "Economic Action and Social Structure: The Problem of Embeddedness." *American Journal of Sociology* 91:481–510.

Grant, Don Sherman. 1992. "Sub-National Social Structures of Accumulation: New Business Investment Across the American States, 1970–1985." Presented at the meeting of the American Sociological Association, Pittsburgh, PA, August 20–24.

Gray, Virginia and David Lowery. 1990. "The Corporatist Foundations of State Industrial Policy." *Social Science Quarterly* 71:3–24.

Green, William C. 1990. "Constitutional Dimensions of State Industrial Recruitment." Pp. 53–83 in *The Politics of Industrial Recruitment*, edited by Ernest J. Yanarella and William C. Green. New York: Greenwood.

Griffin, Larry T., Michael E. Wallace, and Beth A. Rubin. 1986. "Capitalist Resistance to the Organization of Labor Before the New Deal." *American Sociological Review* 51:147–67.

Gunn, Christopher and Hazel Dayton Gunn. 1991. *Reclaiming Capital: Democratic Initiatives and Community Development*. Ithaca, NY: Cornell University Press.

Handbook of Labor Statistics. Various years. Washington, DC: Bureau of Labor Statistics.

Hansen, Susan B. 1990. "Industrial Policies in American States: Historical and Comparative Perspectives." Pp. 3–22 in *The Politics of Industrial Recruitment*, edited by E. J. Yanarella and W. C. Green. New York: Greenwood.

Harrison, Bennett and Barry Bluestone. 1988. *The Great U-Turn: Corporate Restructuring and the Polarization of America*. New York: Basic Books.

Harvey, David. 1989. *The Condition of Postmodernity*. Cambridge, MA: Blackwell.

Hill, Richard C. 1989. "Industrial Restructuring, State Intervention and Uneven Development in the United States and Japan." Pp. 60–85 in *Beyond the City Limits: Urban Policy and Economic Restructuring in Comparative Perspective*, edited by John Logan and Todd Swanstrom. Philadelphia: Temple University Press.

Hill, Richard, Michael Indegaard, and Kuniko Fujita. 1989. "Flat Rock, Home of Mazda: The Social Impact of a Japanese Company on an American Community." Pp. 69–131 in *The Auto Industry Ahead: Who's Driving?* edited by Peter Arnesan. Ann Arbor: University of Michigan-Center for Japanese Studies.

Houghland, James G., Jr. 1991. *Public Perceptions of Central Kentucky Communities and the Impact of Toyota Motor Manufacturing*. Mimeo, University of Kentucky, Center for Developmental Change, July.

———. 1993. "Community-Industry Accommodation: The Case of Toyota in Central Kentucky." Presented at the annual meeting of the North Central Sociological Association, Toledo, Ohio.

Howes, Candace. 1991a. "Transplants No Cure." *Dollars and Sense* 168:16–20.

———. 1991b. "The Benefits of Youth: The Role of Japanese Fringe Benefit Policies in the Restructuring of the U.S. Motor Vehicle Industry." *International Contributions of Labour Studies* 1:113–32.

———. 1993. "Are Japanese Transplants Restoring U.S. Competitiveness or Dumping Their Social Problems in the U.S. Market?" Paper presented at the "Lean Production" Conference, Wayne State University, Detroit, May 20–22.

Johnson, Chalmers. 1982. *MITI and the Japanese Miracle*. Stanford: Stanford University Press.

Katzenstein, Peter J. 1985. *Small States in World Markets*. Ithaca, NY: Cornell University Press.

Kenney, Martin and Richard Florida. 1993. *Beyond Mass Production: The Japanese System and Its Transfer to the United States.* New York: Oxford University Press.

Koebel, C. Theodore, Michael L. Price, Ivan Lee Weir, John P. Nelson, Julia Ingrid Lane, George M. Chapman, and Charles A. Williams III. 1987. *Impacts of the Toyota Plant on Scott County, Kentucky.* Mimeo, Urban Affairs Study Center, University of Louisville.

Leicht, Kevin T. and J. Craig Jenkins. 1991. "The New Corporatism: State-level Economic Development Policy as a Capital Accumulation Strategy." Presented at the 1991 meeting of the Midwest Sociological Society, May, Des Moine, Iowa, April 11–14.

Lincoln, James and Arne Kalleberg. 1985. "Work Organization and Workforce Commitment: A Study of Plants and Employees in the U.S. and Japan." *American Sociological Review* 50:738–60.

Lindblom, Charles. 1977. *Politics and Markets.* New York: Basic Books.

Little, J. S. 1980. "Foreign Direct Investment in the United States: Recent Locational Choices of Foreign Manufacturers." *New England Economic Review.* Boston: Federal Reserve Bank of Boston.

Logan, John R. and Harvey Molotch. 1987. *Urban Fortunes: The Political Economy of Place.* Berkeley: University of California Press.

March, Robert M. 1993. *Working for a Japanese Company: Insights into the Multicultural Workplace.* New York: Kodansha.

Markusen, Ann R. 1987. *Regions: The Economics and Politics of Territory.* Totowa, NJ: Rowman and Littlefield.

McKenzie, Richard B. 1984. *Fugitive Industry: The Economics and Politics of Deindustrialization.* San Francisco: Pacific Institute for Public Policy Research.

Mid-America Project, Inc. 1991. *Keiretsu, USA.* Versailes, KY.

Miller, John and Ramon Castellblanch. 1988. "Does Manufacturing Matter?" *Dollars and Sense* (October):6–8.

Milward, H. Brinton and Heidi H. Newman. 1989. "State Incentive Packages and the Industrial Location Decision." *Economic Development Quarterly* 3:203–22.

Molotch, Harvey. 1976. "The American City as a Growth Machine: Toward a Political Economy of Place." *American Journal of Sociology* 82:309–30.

Molotch, Harvey and John Logan. 1984. "Tensions in the Growth Machine: Overcoming Resistance to Value-Free Development." *Social Problems* 3(June):483–99.

National Association of Japan-America Societies. 333 E. 47th Street, New York.

National Directory of State Agencies. 1989. Gaithersburg, MD: Cambridge Information Group Directories.

Office of Technology Assessment. 1986. *Technology and Structural Unemployment: Reemploying Displaced Adults.* Washington, DC: Congress of the United States.

Osborne, David. 1988. *Laboratories of Democracy.* Boston: Harvard Business School Press.

Perrucci, Carolyn C., Robert Perrucci, Dena B. Targ, and Harry R. Targ. 1988. *Plant Closings: International Context and Social Costs.* Hawthorne, NY: Aldine de Gruyter.

———. 1991. "The Impact of Plant Closings on Workers and Their Families in Declining and Expanding Local Economies." Presented at the 86th Annual

Meeting of the American Sociological Association, Cincinnati, Ohio, August 23–27.

Perrucci, Robert. 1989. "The Political Economy of Foreign Transplants: The Case of Japanese Auto Investment." Presented at the annual meeting of the American Sociological Association, San Francisco, August 10–15.

Perrucci, Robert and Bonnie Lewis. 1989. "Interorganizational Relations and Community Influence Structure: A Replication and Extension." *Sociological Quarterly* 30:205–23.

Perrucci, Robert and Madhavi Patel. 1990. "Local Media Images of Japanese Automobile Investment in Indiana and Kentucky." Pp. 136–152 in *The Politics of Industrial Recruitment*, edited by E. J. Yanarella and W. C. Green. New York: Greenwood.

Perrucci, Robert and Mark Pilisuk. 1970. "Leaders and Ruling Elites: The Interorganizational Bases of Community Power." *American Sociological Review* 35:1040–57.

Piore, Michael J. and Charles F. Sabel. 1984. *The Second Industrial Divide.* New York: Basic Books.

Piven, Francis Fox and Richard Cloward. 1972. *Regulating the Poor.* New York: Random House.

Rachlin, Allen. 1988. *News as Hegemonic Reality.* New York: Basic Books.

Rapoport, Carla. 1991. "Why Japan Keeps Winning." *Fortune* (July 15):76–85.

Reich, Robert B. 1983. *The Next American Frontier.* New York: Times Books.

———. 1990. "Who Is Us?" *Harvard Business Review* 90:53–64.

———. 1993. "Workers of the World, Get Smart." *New York Times*, National Edition, July 20, p. A15.

Romanelli, Elaine. 1989. "Environments and Strategies of Organization Start-Up: Effects on Early Survival." *Administrative Science Quarterly* 34:369–87.

Sabel, Charles F. 1993. "Social Democratic Trade Unions and Politics." Pp. 137–65 in *Economic Restructuring and Emerging Patterns of Industrial Relations*, edited by S. R. Sleigh. Kalamazoo, MI: Upjohn Institute.

Salisbury, Robert H. 1979. "Why No Corporatism in America?" Pp. 213–30 in *Trends Toward Corporatist Intermediation*, edited by Phillipe C. Schmitter and Gerhard Lehmbruch. Beverly Hills: Sage.

Schmitter, Phillipe C. 1979. "Still The Century of Corporatism?" Pp. 7–52 in *Trends Toward Corporatist Intermediation*, edited by Phillipe C. Schmitter and Gerhard Lehmbruch. Beverly Hills: Sage.

Schumpeter, Joseph. 1939. *Business Cycles.* New York: McGraw Hill.

Schudson, Michael. 1978. *Discovering the News: A Social History of American Newspapers.* New York: Basic Books.

Schwartz, Michael and Frank Romo. 1992. "The Uncomfortable Marriage between International Capitalism and Regional Political Economies." Paper presented at the meeting of the American Sociological Association, Pittsburgh, August.

Seeman, Esther Millon. 1992. "Panel Remarks." P. 45 in *Global Partners: Local Communities and Japanese Transplants*, edited by Margaret Chapman and Brian McCullough. Bloomington: Illinois Wesleyan University.

Shaiken, Harvey. 1984. *Work Transformed: Automation and Labor in the Computer Age.* New York: Holt, Rinehart and Winston.

Smith, Michael P. 1987. "Global Capital Restructuring and Local Political Crises." Pp. 234–50 in Global Restructuring and Territorial Development, edited by Jeffrey Henderson and Manuel Castells. Beverly Hills: Sage.

State Elective Officials and the Legislatures. 1993–1994. Lexington, KY: Council of State Governments.

State Information Book. 1987–1988. Rockville, MD: INFAX Corporation.

Stouffer, Samuel. 1950. *The American Soldier*. Princeton, NJ: Princeton University Press.

Summers, Gene F. 1984. "Preface to Deindustrialization: Restructuring the Economy." *Annals of the American Academy of Political and Social Science* 475(September):9–14.

Tolchin, Martin and Susan Tolchin. 1988. *Buying into America: How Foreign Money Is Changing the Face of Our Nation*. New York: Times Books.

Tuchman, Gaye. 1972. "Objectivity as Strategic Ritual: An Examination of Newsmen's Notions of Objectivity." *American Journal of Sociology* 77:660–79.

———. 1978. *Making News: A Study in Construction of Reality*. New York: Free Press.

U.S. Department of Commerce, Bureau of Economic Analysis. 1989. *Business Statistics, 1961–88*. Washington, DC: U.S. Government Printing Office.

Wallace, Michael and Joyce Rothschild. 1988. *Research in Politics and Society, Vol. 3, Deindustrialization and the Restructuring of American Industry*. Greenwich, CT: JAI.

Wenum, John and Margaret Chapman. 1992. "Community Impacts of Auto Transplants." Presented at a conference on Global Partners: Local Communities and Japanese Transplants, Illinois Wesleyan University, October 22–24.

Wilson, Graham K. 1982. "Why Is There No Corporatism in the United States?" Pp. 219–36 in *Patterns of Corporatist Policy-Making*, edited by Gerhard Lehmbruch and Phillipe C. Schmitter. Beverly Hills: Sage.

Womack, James P., Daniel T. Jones, and Daniel Roos. 1990. *The Machine That Changed the World*. New York: Rawson Associates.

Yanarella, Ernest J. and William C. Green (eds.). 1990. *The Politics of Industrial Recruitment: Japanese Automobile Investment and Economic Development in the American States*. New York: Greenwood.

Yoshida, Mamoru. 1987. *Japanese Direct Manufacturing Investment in the United States*. New York: Praeger.

Young, Brigitte. 1990. "Does the American Dairy Industry Fit the Meso-Corporatist Model?" *Political Studies* 38:72–82.

Index